The CaReeR CowaRd's Guide™ to
Changing Careers

Sensible Strategies for Overcoming Job Search Fears

Works
America's Career Publisher

Katy Piotrowski, M.Ed.

The Career Coward's Guide to Changing Careers

© 2008 by Katy Piotrowski

Published by JIST Works, an imprint of JIST Publishing, Inc.
8902 Otis Avenue
Indianapolis, IN 46216-1033
Phone: 1-800-648-JIST   Fax: 1-800-JIST-FAX   E-mail: info@jist.com

Visit our Web site at **www.jist.com** for information on JIST, free job search tips, book chapters, and ordering instructions for our many products!

> Quantity discounts are available for JIST books. Have future editions of JIST books automatically delivered to you on publication through our convenient standing order program. Please call our Sales Department at 1-800-648-5478 for a free catalog and more information.

Trade Product Manager: Lori Cates Hand
Cover Designer: Trudy Coler
Illustrator: Chris Sabatino
Interior Designer: Amy Peppler Adams
Page Layout: Toi Davis
Proofreaders: Linda Seifert, Jeanne Clark
Indexer: Cheryl Lenser

Printed in the United States of America
12 11 10 09 08 07   9 8 7 6 5 4 3 2 1

Library of Congress Cataloging-in-Publication Data

Piotrowski, Katy, 1962-
    The career coward's guide to changing careers : sensible strategies for overcoming job search fears / by Katy Piotrowski.
        p. cm.
    Includes index.
    ISBN 978-1-59357-390-4 (alk. paper)
1. Career changes. 2. Job hunting. I. Title.
    HF5384.P56 2008
    650.14--dc22
                                    2007022549

About This Book

You're seriously considering changing careers. Wow...good for you! But it feels pretty scary, doesn't it? You're probably worrying about a lot of things right now, like, "How will I identify a new career—and research it—to make sure that it's right for me? And how will I put together and implement a doable, successful career-change plan that allows me to maintain my life while achieving my career goals?" It's a little overwhelming, isn't it?

But today's your lucky day, because in your hands you hold a proven how-to guide that will show you *exactly* how to do it—one successful baby step at a time. *The Career Coward's Guide to Changing Careers* will show you *exactly* how to discover exciting, satisfying new careers that fit your unique interests, lifestyle, and skills, and then show you how to check them out to make sure they're right for you. From there, you'll learn how to put together an achievable plan that will allow you to bridge successfully into your rewarding new career.

Does it work. Oh, yes! The process described in *The Career Coward's Guide to Changing Careers* has been tested on hundreds of people just like you (and most of them were a little scared, too!) over the last 15 years.

Those career changers have paved the way for you to make use of the surefire processes and steps that worked for them.

Still seem a little scary? That's understandable. So I've designed this book to cater to people just like you—someone who's feeling excited...but a little unsure about how the whole process works. Take a peek inside: There are "Panic Points" throughout the book that highlight—and provide solutions for—the steps in the career-change process that seem especially frightening.

There are also several real-life stories about successful career changers, to inspire you and help show you the way. Plus, there are tons of other great advice that will teach you how to reduce your risk and increase your chances of achieving true career-change success. Sound good? C'mon! Let's get started, and make this important career change a reality for you. Your first step is just a few pages away.

—Katy P.

Dedication

*To John, who gave me my first opportunity
as a career counselor. And to my career-change
clients, who bravely showed me the way.*

Contents

Acknowledgments

Creating a career I love—and as a result, this book—has required the support of many people: First, my parents, who have always believed in me. Thanks, Mom and Dad! To my wise and encouraging career-counseling instructors at Colorado State University, particularly Nat Kees and Rich Feller. To the career-counseling gurus who continue to inspire and drive my work with their wonderful teachings: Richard Bolles, Daniel Porot, Bernard Haldane, Herminia Ibarra, and Richard Knowdell. To John, who gave me my first chance to be a "real" career counselor. To my husband, Pete, who tirelessly says, "You can do this. I believe in you." Pete, you are my rock and my best friend. To my talented support team at JIST, who continue to make the business of book writing and publishing rewarding and fun. And most importantly, to my clients, who allow me the honor of being a part of their journey toward achieving career happiness.

Tame the Coward and Change Careers!

You're ready.

For a long time now, you've thought about changing careers. You want to find work that's more meaningful and will make better use of your skills. You want to wake up each day *excited*, knowing that your work is helping you accomplish what you want out of life.

You're really, *really* ready.

But you're also really, really scared. Changing careers seems overwhelming. What do you choose? And how do you move into a new career in a way that doesn't totally disrupt your life? How do you put together the thousands of details to make a smooth transition into a better work situation?

On their own, these questions are challenging enough. But chances are you're also wrestling with a tiny voice inside of you that keeps whispering, "What if it doesn't work? Wouldn't it be better to just keep doing what you're already doing and not risk failing? Do you *really* think you can succeed in another career? What if you're only good at what you're doing now?"

Or worst of all, "What if you try, and fail, and then you won't even have your career-change hopes to hold onto anymore?"

If this sounds like you, then most likely you *are* a Career Coward— you know you're capable of greater career successes, but you feel terrified and paralyzed to take steps to move forward because you're afraid you'll fail or look like a fool. It's a frustrating spot to be in.

Yet you don't need to keep living your life as a Career Coward. This book, *The Career Coward's Guide to Changing Careers*, was written to help you overcome your fear of changing careers, and ultimately succeed in achieving your goals.

How to Use This Book to Achieve Your Career-Change Goals

The Career Coward's Guide to Changing Careers walks you through a proven, step-by-step process for overcoming your fears and creating the career life you want. Each chapter in this book provides you with techniques that have been tried, tested, and perfected on thousands of other Career Cowards. And to make this valuable information even more fun and easy to use, each chapter includes an at-a-glance "Risk It or Run From It" status box, providing you the following vital information:

- **Risk Rating:** From "no risk at all" to "this is a deal breaker!" you'll quickly see how harmless or hazardous each step will be.

- **Payoff Potential:** Find out what's in it for you if you *do* decide to take the risk and complete the step. The payoff may be enough to push you through any fear holding you back.

- **Time to Complete:** Whether it's a few minutes, a few hours, or longer, you'll know in advance how much time each activity will take.

- **Bailout Strategy:** Absolutely refuse to put in the time or take the risk for a particular step? You have other options; find out what they are.

- **The "20 Percent Extra" Edge:** Learn how braving the recommended steps will give you a significant advantage over your competition.

- **"Go For It!" Bonus Activity:** Feeling really courageous? Push your success even further with this suggested activity.

Each information-packed chapter also includes

- A **"How To"** section, which provides clear, motivating instructions for each activity.

- Information about **"Why It's Worth Doing,"** which helps you understand the purpose behind each career-change recommendation.

- **"Panic Point!"** highlights, which point out and troubleshoot areas Career Cowards find especially challenging.

- An encouraging **"Career Champ Profile,"** which describes a real-life example of a Career Coward who succeeded after conquering a challenging career-change fear.

- The **"Core Courage Concept,"** which boils down the chapter's key points into an inspiring message.

- And a **"Confidence Checklist,"** which provides you an at-a-glance review of the chapter's primary action items.

As you move through the chapters of this book, you'll learn how to implement and succeed with the following proven career-change action plan:

- You'll begin by identifying several career areas that offer a great match for your talents, skills, interests, and values. This is a fun, step-by-step process guaranteed to deliver a number of excellent new-career possibilities that are just right for you, including several ideas you might not have considered before.

- You'll then research the careers that look most appealing, which allows you to choose the best career options for you while also determining a successful strategy for implementing your career change. As a bonus, this research will connect you with experts in the fields you're investigating through inspiring, confidence-boosting activities. And along the way, you'll implement a number of fun, low-risk career experiments that will help you confirm that "Yes!", a particular career specialty is in fact a great match for you.

- These steps will then lead you smoothly into defining and executing a successful new-career execution plan, helping you land your first opportunities in your new career field.

- And throughout the entire process, you'll prove to yourself again and again that you can overcome that annoying, power-stealing Career Coward that's been holding you back—and ultimately achieve the career success and satisfaction you desire.

Feeling excited? Ready to move on? Great! Now find out how the techniques described in this book helped a Career Coward just like you.

Career Champ Profile: Gabe

Gabe had developed a successful career in manufacturing. Over time, he'd risen through the ranks from assembler, to technician, to shift supervisor, and eventually to director of the entire manufacturing operation for a pharmaceutical company. He was highly skilled and well paid for his expertise.

Yet he *hated* his work. The pharmaceutical industry seemed to be in constant flux. His employer companies were frequently getting acquired, merging, relocating, or going out of business altogether. From one week to the next, Gabe worried that he wouldn't have a job. He also found the work unfulfilling. He spent more and more time in frustrating meetings, and felt that even if he had a good idea to offer, there was too much red tape to cut through to ever have his idea implemented.

For years, Gabe thought about changing careers. He longed to move into work that would be more meaningful and make better use of his skills. Yet every time the idea of changing careers came into his mind, a little voice (Gabe's Career Coward) would pipe up with a comment like, "Yeah, and how will you pay your bills? You have a family and responsibilities! And what if you're really only good at manufacturing? What if you can't succeed in another line of work?" Gabe's Career Coward would quickly shut down his hopes of changing careers.

But one day, Gabe decided to stop letting his Career Coward run his life, and to find a way to truly make his career change happen. He learned about and implemented many of the techniques described in this book.

For instance, he began by identifying potential careers that would make good use of his talents and interests, as well as allow him to live the lifestyle he wanted. He then carefully researched them by interviewing people who were working in those specialties and executing low-risk "career experiments" to see whether he'd actually enjoy the work he was considering. Gabe determined that a career in sales within the environmental industry would make great use of his talents in building successful relationships, while also allowing him to apply his scientific background. And because he lacked specific skills in selling, he took classes in sales to build his expertise.

Over time, Gabe began to get a clear picture of how he could accomplish his new career goals. As he developed his plan, his confidence grew, and his Career Coward's voice grew more and more faint. Eventually Gabe implemented a job search plan to find work in his new field. Ultimately, Gabe's career-change activities led to an excellent result. Within a few months he landed a job as an account manager with an environmental waste-management organization. Even though Gabe felt like a newbie for the first few months in his new job, he realized almost immediately that the change was giving him much greater career satisfaction.

Yet Gabe's career change still wasn't complete. To overcome the frustration of relying on one employer for his paycheck, Gabe also decided to start a sideline business. He and a friend purchased a small company that manufactures organic soaps and lotions. On nights and weekends, Gabe and his partner now produce products and fill orders. Eventually Gabe's business may become his full-time work, but for now he likes the security that comes with having multiple income sources.

At this stage in his life, Gabe is ecstatic about his work. His skills and talents are being put to good use, and he's motivated and energized each morning when he wakes up. Even though it took time and effort to accomplish, Gabe views his career change as one of the greatest accomplishments in his life. He conquered his Career Coward and created a career situation he loves.

Feeling inspired to achieve this same kind of success for yourself? Great! Let's get started.

Part 1

Building Blocks for Your Career Change

Chapter 1

Discover Your Natural Talents and Best Skills

We've all been blessed with talents (whether or not we recognize them), and throughout our lives, we each develop a unique set of skills. When we make good use of those talents and skills, we feel great about ourselves. So what are yours? This chapter will help you create an accurate and inspiring list of your best abilities.

Risk It or Run From It?

- **Risk Rating:** Low (plus, it's fun!).

- **Payoff Potential:** Humongous! This is one of the key building blocks to your future career happiness.

- **Time to Complete:** An hour or so.

- **Bailout Strategy:** If you already know what you're great at, and are confident that you can create a list of 5 to 10 of your best talents and skills, write the list and skip the exercises.

- **The "20 Percent Extra" Edge:** A clear idea of your best talents and skills allows Career Cowards to focus their time and energy in areas that can produce the highest payoff. This

(continued)

(continued)

> strategy allows you to get where you want to go faster, with fewer frustrations (and a happier result!).
>
> • **"Go For It!" Bonus Activity:** Show the Talents and Skills survey to two or three people who believe in you and know you well, and ask for their input.

How to Identify Your Best Talents and Skills

Wish you had a defined list of your best talents and skills to help you define a more satisfying career, but struggle with which abilities are truly your greatest (or if you even have any to offer at all)? The following step-by-step process will help you recall the skills and talents that give you the most pleasure. Then you can develop a prioritized list to guide you in your career-change choices.

Understand What Qualifies as a Talent or Skill

A talent is a natural ability that is valued by others and that comes easily to you. Often, our talents are abilities that we're born with, and that become apparent as we go through life. For instance, my daughter has a talent for remembering strings of digits, such as phone numbers. She can see a phone number one time, and later recall it accurately. This is an ability she was born with. She didn't get a bachelor's degree in number-recall to learn how to memorize numbers—it's just a talent that she's always possessed.

A skill is an ability that you've developed over time through use, practice, and education. Although you might not have been born with this ability, you have developed it to a level of expertise that surpasses the abilities of most other people. My husband, for example, is a skilled computer programmer. Although he didn't arrive in this world able to program computers, he completed two engineering degrees and has spent thousands of hours mastering this ability, to the point that he's now highly skilled in programming.

An activity that may be a talent for one person, as in, "She was born with the ability to sing like an angel," may be a skill that another person had to develop, such as, "He took voice lessons for several years to become an accomplished baritone." For this reason, I'll be using the terms "talents" and "skills" interchangeably.

We all have talents and skills, even if we're hesitant to admit them or have a hard time recognizing them in ourselves.

Panic Point! Career Cowards often worry, "In the grand scheme of things, how do my skills and talents truly stack up against other people? Can I honestly say that my talent or skill is good enough to be called a strength? And if I do say that I'm strong in a particular ability, who's to say that the Talent and Skill Review Committee (in case they exist) won't come knocking at my door to make me prove it—exposing me as an imposter?"

It is difficult to know for certain that, without a doubt, you're blessed with a particular talent or skill. Tests that determine your level of expertise in a specific skill or talent area don't exist for most abilities. But although an exam to certify your strength in say, organization, doesn't exist, there are clues that can provide evidence of your strengths in particular talent and skill areas. Enough of those clues can help you arrive at the conclusion that yes, a skill or talent is one that you can boast as being yours.

And because talents and skills are such a vital component in identifying and executing a successful career change, it's worth the struggle to define them. The following activities will help you articulate your skills and talents—and then prove to yourself that they're truly yours to boast about.

Review Your Talent and Skill History

Throughout your life, you've had a chance to try your hand at a variety of talent and skill areas. And you probably discovered you *didn't* possess a natural inclination in many of those areas. Playing piano was one of those experiences for me. Even though I took lessons for a year, and practiced the recommended number of times each week, my mother and I both agreed that it would be better for me to leave that activity alone.

Yet as a child, there were probably several pursuits that did come naturally—or seem especially enjoyable—to you. You may have participated on a sports team, made crafts at summer camp, or organized games with neighborhood buddies. Within your family, you may have always been the one who orchestrated get-togethers, researched needed information, or repaired broken items.

You've probably also received feedback from others on what they believe to be your strengths. Your Aunt Margie may have said, "You are so 'creative!'" or your teacher may have complimented you on your carefulness and attention to detail. Bosses have probably given you feedback, too, either directly through comments such as, "You're great at resolving customer problems," or indirectly by repeatedly assigning you certain tasks.

So what are some of those talents and skills you've demonstrated—or been recognized for—throughout your life? Make a list of at least five for each of these topic areas:

- Activities you recall spending time on and enjoying as a child.

  _____

  _____

  _____

  _____

  _____

- Subjects that came easily to you and were fun for you in school.

  _____

  _____

_____

_____

_____

- Things that you're "known" for within your family, as in "Sarah's always been so good at _X_."

_____

_____

_____

_____

- Types of assignments, or requests for assistance, that family members and employers frequently ask of you.

_____

_____

_____

_____

Create this list and then set it aside.

Recall Your "Great-Feeling" Experiences

In addition to the activities you were drawn to as a child and the qualities you've been praised for at home, school, and work, there are most likely several instances in your life when you felt great as you made use of a particular skill or talent.

For instance, I experienced my earliest "great-feeling" memory when I played the part of the Grinch in our grade school's production of _How the Grinch Stole Christmas_. I clearly remember how wonderful I felt performing—entertaining the audience, speaking my lines, acting out the scenes.

In college, I recall several great-feeling experiences tied to home-work in one of my advertising classes. I loved the assignments: "Design a logo for Company *X*." "Write a brochure for Business *Y*." "Develop an ad campaign for Organization *Z*." I would happily get lost in the projects for hours, and I even won an award for an electric-company ad series I designed my senior year in college.

My first job out of college provided other "great-feeling" opportunities. My employer wanted to send holiday gifts to 300 of its best customers. I created and executed a "12 Days of Christmas" program—sending special cards and gifts to those 300 customers over a 12-day period (thank heaven for FedEx!)—and loved every second of conceptualizing, organizing, and executing the project.

Now, my great-feeling experiences come most often from presenting career seminars, working with clients, and writing about career top-ics. I remember, for instance, sitting in our family van at a hotel parking lot one rainy afternoon (while my husband played guitar for a wedding inside the hotel), pecking away on my laptop writing my preceding *Career Coward* book, and feeling about as happy and satis-fied as I imagine a person can feel.

How about you? When in your life have you had great-feeling expe-riences that involved use of a particular skill or talent? To help you remember some instances, consider the following times in your life. Aim to recall a total of at least five great-feeling experiences. Jot down a few notes about each experience for reference later.

- **Early-childhood experiences:** Working on particular assign-ments, participating in certain activities, spending time with hobbies or projects on your own.

    _____

    _____

    _____

- **Middle school or high school experiences:** Developing skills that interested you, seeking out opportunities to learn and master more about activities you enjoyed.

  _____

  _____

- **College or early work experiences:** Trying your hand at different tasks, learning new skills, successfully handling work duties or special projects.

  _____

  _____

- **Hobbies and outside-of-work experiences:** Pursuits you seek out in your free time because they interest you and bring you so much pleasure.

  _____

  _____

- **Later career and life experiences:** Times when you've felt deeply satisfied because of your involvement in a particular project, task, or activity.

  _____

  _____

Consider Your Untapped Talents and Skills

Although there are many talents and skills you've been exposed to in your life, there are also many more that you haven't yet experienced. These may be areas where you have potential to excel, but you haven't had a chance to experience the ability well enough to know for sure.

For instance, in college I once took a computer-programming class. For one assignment, we had to write a program that would allow only a certain number of people into a bar at once. As people left the bar, more people could enter. I have positive memories of working on that project. It was the only experience I've ever had with programming. Since then, I've wondered whether I would have enjoyed programming if I'd chosen to develop the skill further.

What skills or talents are still waiting in the wings for you, hoping to be considered and developed? Make a list of any that come to mind for you as you think about the following, aiming for a minimum of three or more talent or skill areas you may want to develop:

- Talents or skills you've admired in others and thought, "I might be pretty good at that myself."

- Abilities that you've had an introductory exposure to—and enjoyed—but haven't developed further.

- Skill-development goals you've had in mind for yourself but haven't yet accomplished.

_____

_____

_____

_____

_____

_____

Measure Your Use of Talents and Skills

Now that you've thought through your talent and skills history, recalled several "great-feeling" experiences in your life, and taken into consideration abilities you may eventually want to develop, look at the following list and circle all the skills or talents that have come up related to the lists you've made.

Acting

Administering programs

Advising people

Advocating

Analyzing

Assembling things

Athletic abilities

Attending to detail

Auditing information or processes

Budgeting

Building teams

Building trust

Calculating data

Classifying information

Coaching

Collaborating

Collecting information

Compiling data or things

Conceptualizing ideas

Constructing things

Coordinating

Correcting errors

Counseling

Creating crafts

Decision making

Defining needs

Delegating

Designing

Disseminating information

Distributing

Drawing

Editing

Encouraging others

Enforcing policies

Estimating

Evaluating

Fixing things

Forecasting

Fund-raising

Handling details

Helping others

Hosting

Implementing new ideas

Inspecting

Interpreting languages or information

Interviewing

Inventing ideas or things

Investigating

Leading

Maintaining information

Managing

Managing conflict

Managing time

Motivating

Negotiating

Operating equipment

Organizing

Performing

Persuading

Planning

Programming

Promoting activities or people

Promoting change

Proposing ideas

Providing information

Public speaking

Researching

Screening information and people

Selling

Selling ideas or products

Servicing	Supervising	Training
Solving problems	Teaching	Writing

Next, review the talents and skills you've circled and place a checkmark by each item every time it was used in one of the examples you listed earlier. For instance, the skill "teaching" may have shown up with one high school example (when you were asked to tutor a classmate in math), one childhood example (when you organized a pretend classroom and invited your neighborhood friends), one outside-of-work example (when you volunteered to teach reading skills to some children in a community program), and one work example (when your boss assigned you to teach a coworker how to use the company's database program)—so that skill would have four checkmarks beside it.

Be liberal with your checkmarks at this point. For example, if you're wondering, "Training seems a lot like teaching to me, so should I check both?" the answer is yes. Or sometimes Career Cowards try to decide whether they were truly making use of a particular skill (but they're pretty sure that they were). If this is how you're feeling about a skill, go ahead and check it. You'll have an opportunity to further refine your skills and talents list as we go along, but for now, check freely!

Prioritize Your Top Skill and Talent Areas

Now add up your checkmarks for each skill and create a list of skills and talents prioritized by number of checkmarks listed. For instance, if you have the greatest number of checkmarks beside "fixing things," "solving problems," and "budgeting" (let's say, six checkmarks beside each), those three skills will be at the top of your Talents and Skills list. Beside "supervising," "calculating data," and "analyzing," you might have five checkmarks, so you would list those next, and so on. Create a list of 10 to 20 skills and talents with the greatest number of checkmarks. If it makes sense, feel free to combine certain skills that to you seem very similar, such as "teaching" and "training."

Put Strengths to the Evidence Test

Following is a worksheet that will enable you to collect concrete evidence of your proficiency in specific skill and talent areas. Here's how to complete it:

1. At the top of the worksheet, fill in your top-priority skills and talents from the prioritized list you just created. (Photocopy the test if you want to measure more than eight skills or talents.)

2. For each talent or skill, read through the statements on the left side of the worksheet and give yourself one point for each statement to which you can answer "yes."

3. Complete this evaluation for each of your top-priority skills and talents.

4. Tally up the total number of points for each talent or skill area at the bottom of the worksheet.

Skills and Talents Evidence Test

TALENT/SKILL	EVIDENCE OF EXPERTISE						
Personal Talent/ Skill Experiences							
"I frequently wish that I could spend more time using this skill."	☐	☐	☐	☐	☐	☐	☐
"I use this skill often, even in my free time."	☐	☐	☐	☐	☐	☐	☐
"I can recall more than 10 instances when I have used this skill successfully."	☐	☐	☐	☐	☐		☐
"I can recall using this skill a number of times, even in my early childhood."	☐	☐	☐	☐	☐	☐	☐
Input from Others Regarding Your Talent/Skill							
"Family members have repeatedly praised me on my ability with this skill."	☐	☐	☐	☐	☐	☐	☐

"I am often asked by others to perform this skill, either for pay or as a favor."	☐	☐	☐	☐	☐	☐	☐	☐
"Coworkers or team members have frequently complimented me on my knack for this skill."	☐	☐	☐	☐	☐	☐	☐	☐

Concrete Evidence of Talent/Skill

"I have received professional training or education in this area."	☐	☐	☐	☐	☐	☐	☐	☐
"I have been paid to perform this skill."	☐	☐	☐	☐	☐	☐	☐	☐
"I have been evaluated on this skill and received high marks."	☐	☐	☐	☐	☐	☐	☐	☐
"I have received an award for this skill."	☐	☐	☐	☐	☐	☐	☐	☐
TOTAL	—	—	—	—	—	—	—	—

For the last step, create a final list of your top 10 to 20 skills and talents, prioritized in order of their Evidence Test scores. Congratulations! You've just created and measured a list of your top talent and skills areas. Hang onto this list for future reference; you'll use it in a future chapter.

My Top Skills and Talents

1. _____

2. _____

3. _____

4. _____

5. _____

6. _____

7. _____

8. _____

9. _____

10. _____

11. _____

12. _____

13. _____

14. _____

15. _____

16. _____

17. _____

18. _____

19. _____

20. _____

Why It's Worth Doing

Defining a list of your top strengths enables you to build your career-change efforts on a solid foundation of the talents and skills that are most valuable to you. Although the process of articulating and prioritizing your skills and talents can make you squirm a little, the list—once created—will be one of your most valuable career-change tools, helping to guide you to good-fit career options and ultimately allowing you to spend your time engaged in activities that are most rewarding for you.

Career Champ Profile: Marlee

Marlee was raised in a middle-class household in the '60s and '70s. Her parents gave her a comfortable life and supported her interests. Marlee took gymnastics as a child, participated in several travel activities offered by her church's youth group, served as the assistant editor of her high school's newspaper, and acted in a number of community theater performances. She developed a reputation among her family and friends for being a talented writer and artist. She even wrote and illustrated a number of storybooks as gifts for special friends and family members.

In college, Marlee chose graphic design as her major. She landed a job with an advertising agency after graduation, and was frequently assigned to work with small businesses to develop their logos and advertising materials.

After marrying, she and her husband moved to a different state, and Marlee took work in a retail position at a women's clothing store. For years, she enjoyed her retail work, especially creating attractive displays and developing fun promotional programs to boost clothing sales. Eventually, though, the unpredictable work schedule, requiring her to frequently work nights and weekends, caused Marlee to consider a career change. Yet even though she was motivated to improve her situation, it took more than three years to actually begin making a change. Marlee dragged her feet because she worried that she really had no valuable skills or talents to apply to anything other than retail.

As a first step, Marlee agreed to take an inventory of her former experiences and future hopes, resulting in this list of her top skill and talent areas, prioritized in this order:

Designing things (seven checkmarks)

Creating crafts (seven checkmarks)

Writing (six checkmarks)

Constructing things (five checkmarks)

Implementing new ideas (five checkmarks)

Promoting ideas or people (five checkmarks)

Athletic abilities (four checkmarks)

Hosting (three checkmarks)

Inventing ideas or things (three checkmarks)

Acting (three checkmarks)

This exercise eventually helped Marlee identify a few career possibilities that she hadn't considered before and that were especially appealing to her: yoga instructor and book cover illustrator. The prospect of moving into a career specialty she loved motivated her to take further steps in her career development. Marlee was on her way!

Core Courage Concept

You know you have strengths. Yet challenging yourself to create a list of your very best talents and skills can feel overwhelming and scary. "Who's to say that I'm truly strong in this area?" you might worry. "And what if I admit that I really do want to use a particular talent or skill, and then later fail?"

Yes, admitting and committing to your talents and skills is a scary step. But it's a step worth risking. Because when you build off of your strengths, you give yourself the advantage of launching your career change from the best possible foundation.

Confidence Checklist

☐ Understand what qualifies as a talent or skill.

☐ Review your talent and skill history.

☐ Recall your "great-feeling" experiences.

☐ Consider your untapped talents and skills.

☐ Measure your use of certain talents and skills

☐ Prioritize your top skill and talent areas.

☐ Put your strengths to the Evidence Test.

Chapter 2

Visualize Your Ideal Career

All of us wish for a satisfied, rewarding life. Yet Career Cowards frequently let their fears get in the way of creating their dream lifestyle. Either they haven't defined their ideal lifestyle clearly enough, or they continue to make decisions that get in the way of realizing their dreams. Whatever might be blocking your way, by the end of this chapter, you will have developed a vision for what you want in your life *and* will have created a list of valuable decision-making guidelines that will help you overcome your fears and achieve it!

Risk It or Run From It?

- **Risk Rating:** Very low. You'll first just imagine what you'd like your ideal life and work to be, and then determine which values and decisions will help you get there.

- **Payoff Potential:** Very high. Defining what you hope to create for yourself—and then determining which values are most important to you—provides you with powerful lifelong planning and decision-making tools.

- **Time to Complete:** 15 to 60 minutes.

(continued)

(continued)

- **Bailout Strategy:** It would be better if you didn't skip this step (it would be like trying to build a house without a blueprint), but if you must bypass it, at least look at the list of values and choose your top 10 to help with decision-making later.

- **The "20 Percent Extra" Edge:** Several studies have shown that if you write down your goals, you greatly increase your chance of achieving them. It's as if by actually writing them down, you program your brain to make them happen.

- **"Go For It!" Bonus Activity:** In addition to jotting down some notes on your ideal work and life, create a collage of your hopes using pictures from magazines to represent the life you'd like to create for yourself.

How to Create a Vision of Your Ideal Career

As a child, I remember dreaming about being famous performer (remember my Grinch experience?). Back then, I remember confessing my dream to a few people—family members, teachers—but very quickly I learned that others were skeptical that my vision was possible. "Lots of people want to be famous, but very few ever make it," they'd say. I remember the sad, sick feeling that crept into my stomach as I heard their words. "Acting is my dream," I'd think to myself, "but maybe it's impossible." So I shoved my hopes to the back of my mind and stopped mentioning them to people. I even stopped trying out for plays at school. Why bother? I told myself. Very few ever really make it....

I even started feeling a little embarrassed about my interest in performing and acting, and started to hide it. I got busy with more practical interests. If I couldn't be in the spotlight, I'd help other people get there. In high school, I got involved with campaigns for fellow classmates who were running for positions on student council, creating posters, buttons, and campaign slogans. It was fun work and I was good at it. That activity led to getting my first degree in advertising, which led to my first career in marketing.

Ironically, however, my life path seems to have brought me back to my first love. Looking for more meaningful work led me to switch careers into career counseling, where I actually get to do quite a bit of acting and performing. Helping clients prepare for interviews, I act the part of an interviewer, pretending to be a hiring manager. In the career workshops and presentations I lead, I love figuring out ways to make my material interesting to the audience, and strive to present it with flair and impact. And even in my volunteer activities, I act. As a Sunday-school teacher I lead a drama class, helping students play the parts of characters in stories.

I've also discovered that based on my interests in life, I'm not really drawn to becoming a world renowned Broadway, television, or film actor. Those specialties would require me to spend too much time away from home, and I'm a chronic homebody. Rather, what seemed appealing to me as a child (but which I didn't have the words to describe at that time) was having the opportunity to present meaningful information in a fun, interesting way—and that's *exactly* what I get to do in my life now!

Richard Bolles, author of *What Color Is Your Parachute?*, believes that we're all put on this planet with a unique set of talents and interests. Those talents and interests are meant to be used in ways that not only bring us satisfaction, but that also benefit the world. There is a general life path that we're intended to follow that will allow us to use those unique talents and interests in many possible ways. My experience with landing on a path where I can make use of my talent for performing, and my interest in sharing meaningful information, is evidence of Bolles' theory in action. And as I've observed the unfolding of my clients' career paths, I believe more and more that through just a little conscious effort and planning, we can all create a satisfying career path experience.

What is your life path meant to look like? Reading this statement may cause you to feel a little panicked.

Panic Point! "I don't *know* what my life path is supposed to look like," the Career Coward in you may be thinking. "That's what this book is supposed to help me figure out!" You're right; this book will help define a better picture of your career path and opportunities. And although at this moment I don't expect you to have a crystal-clear picture of what your path will look like (or ever, for that matter—a fuzzy picture is usually sufficient), I do want you to pay attention to any hints you've had on this subject so far. Like my longtime desire to perform, you most likely have dreams that you've been carrying around for a while.

The following exercise is designed to help you to once again pay attention to those long-term desires. You'll be asked to write your thoughts in response to several questions to help you begin defining pieces of your vision. So push through your feeling of "I don't *know!*" panic and see what might come to mind for you. You may be pleasantly surprised!

Create a Picture of Your Ideal Work and Life

With this exercise, you are going to imagine, in your mind's eye, your ideal work and life situation. Although you may not be able to visualize every exact detail, you will most likely be able to envision your basic hopes for your lifestyle and routine. For just a little while, allow yourself to dream the most desirable situation possible for yourself. Keep in mind that for now, you're only imagining what you'd like to create.

Panic Point! Career Cowards often talk themselves out of their true wishes by thinking, "I'd like for this to happen, but really...what are the chances? Why even write it down?" Remember, your goal at this moment is to visualize your ideal situation. Have faith that later, you'll figure out how to make it happen. (And don't worry...I'll give you some doable steps for that part, too.)

To begin, find a quiet, pleasant place where you can think to yourself without interruptions for 30 minutes or so. It might be on a park bench, at a coffee shop, in your bedroom, or on a walk. Be sure to take along the following list of questions and note-taking materials. Once you're in your peaceful place, tell yourself to set aside the many thoughts and concerns that have been on your mind. You can go back to them again in a little while. But for now, your focus will be on visualizing your ideal career situation.

Ask yourself the following questions and jot down your answers for each. If you're not able to think of an answer to a question right away, ask your mind to mull over it for a while, move on to another question, and then come back to the unanswered question later.

Picture yourself sometime in the future. It could be two years, or ten, or twenty. You want to choose a timeframe that feels far enough out in the future for you to be able to accomplish what you envision for yourself. If, for example, you visualize yourself running a successful small business, plan for however many years you expect it would take you to achieve that goal.

Begin by writing down anything you see in your future picture. For instance, where are you? Are you indoors or outdoors? Is it a different city or country? What do you see around you? Describe the things you see. What's the weather like? What season is it?

Now ask yourself, what are you doing in this picture? What tools and materials are you working with? What do you spend your time talking or thinking about? Which activities give you joy and pleasure? What feels especially meaningful to you? How does your day progress? What new activities do you begin?

In this picture, what topics, issues, or thoughts take your attention much of the time? What problems are you trying to solve, or what goals are you aiming to achieve? What benefits does your expertise create for others? What rewards do *you* receive from your work and activities? How are you compensated?

Other than yourself, who is in your picture? How do you interact with them? What purpose do they serve in your life?

Also, what other pieces of your life exist that are important to you, but aren't in this picture that you're visualizing right now? What hobbies, places, activities, and events are you involved with at different times of the day, week, month, or year? Do you travel from one place to another? If so, where do you go? Who do you see and interact with during those times?

Looking even further into the future, what are your longer-term goals? What are your efforts leading toward? How are you progressing and developing yourself? What are you aiming to achieve ultimately?

Now, reflect on this life that you've created. What decisions have you made that support what is most important and meaningful to you? What values do you honor every day that help you to maintain your sense of respect for yourself and the world? What beliefs and standards do you live by?

Write down as many ideas as possible related to these questions. It may help to begin this exercise, leave it alone for a day or so, and then come back to it when your mind has been able to develop some further insights.

When you've written down as many thoughts as you can (for now, at least), declare it "good enough!" and set it aside.

Panic Point! Your visualization may not be as detailed or crystal-clear as you hoped it might be, but that's okay. Remember that this visualization will continue to evolve and change as you progress along your life and work path.

Uncover the Values Hidden in Your Ideal Situation

From here you're going to look for important clues in the visualization you've just created. Your goal is to identify 10 to 20 values that are most important to you in your ideal work and life. To help with this part of the exercise, refer to the list of values included later in this section. Although it's a pretty long list, you may discover that it doesn't include a value that is important to you, so feel free to add your own values if you want.

To uncover the values hidden in your visualization, read through what you've written, and for each of the specific situations you've described, ask yourself, "What about this particular activity is important to me? Which value (or values) does it support?"

For instance, in one part of my own personal visualization, I picture myself living with my husband in a home along the beach. Each day, I see myself interacting with my husband and visitors (family and close friends who stay in a place nearby), spending part of my day writing and talking on the phone to people in the career counseling world, and taking a few hours to exercise, cook, and read. For one week each month, I picture myself leaving my beach home and traveling somewhere for a career presentation or conference. These are fun, highly rewarding trips for me, for which I'm well compensated.

When I ask myself, "What about these particular activities are important to me?" the following values come to mind:

- **Family:** I've got my family close by (but not right on top of each other!).

- **Creativity:** Writing and giving presentations are hugely satisfying to me because they allow me to play with ideas in a challenging and meaningful way.

- **Advancement:** My aim in talking with people in the career counseling world is to learn new things and develop opportunities to grow.

- **Intimacy:** I see myself spending a good deal of time with my husband each day, while he's also busy with his interests and activities.

- **Expertise:** I like having a topic that I know in depth and can keep mastering.

- **Making a difference:** It's important to me that my work is meaningful to both myself and other people.

- **Security:** My family and I have the financial means to live safely and comfortably.

- **Health:** You know what they say…without it, nothing else matters.

Abundance	Attractiveness	Cleanliness
Acceptance	Availability	Cleverness
Accomplishment	Balance	Closeness
Accuracy	Beauty	Comfort
Achievement	Being the best	Commitment
Activeness	Belonging	Compassion
Adaptability	Bravery	Completion
Adventure	Calmness	Composure
Affection	Camaraderie	Concentration
Affluence	Capability	Confidence
Altruism	Carefulness	Connection
Ambition	Celebrity	Consciousness
Amusement	Challenge	Consistency
Appreciation	Charm	Contentment
Assertiveness	Cheerfulness	Contribution
Attentiveness	Clarity	Control

Conviction	Effectiveness	Focus
Coolness	Efficiency	Freedom
Cooperation	Empathy	Friendliness
Correctness	Encouragement	Frugality
Courage	Endurance	Fun
Courtesy	Energy	Generosity
Craftiness	Enjoyment	Giving
Creativity	Entertainment	Gratitude
Credibility	Enthusiasm	Growth
Cunning	Excellence	Happiness
Curiosity	Excitement	Harmony
Daring	Exhilaration	Health
Decisiveness	Expediency	Heart
Dependability	Expertise	Helpfulness
Determination	Exploration	Heroism
Devoutness	Expressiveness	Honesty
Dexterity	Fairness	Honor
Diligence	Faith	Humility
Discipline	Fame	Humor
Discovery	Family	Independence
Diversity	Fearlessness	Insightfulness
Drive	Fidelity	Inspiration
Duty	Financial	Integrity
Dynamism	independence	Intelligence
Eagerness	Fitness	Intensity
Education	Flexibility	Intimacy

Introversion	Organization	Respect
Intuition	Originality	Richness
Inventiveness	Passion	Sacrifice
Investing	Peace	Security
Joy	Perfection	Self-reliance
Justice	Perkiness	Service
Kindness	Persistence	Sharing
Knowledge	Persuasiveness	Shrewdness
Leadership	Philanthropy	Sincerity
Learning	Popularity	Skillfulness
Liberation	Power	Solitude
Liveliness	Practicality	Spirit
Logic	Pragmatism	Spirituality
Longevity	Precision	Spontaneity
Love	Privacy	Stability
Loyalty	Proactivity	Strength
Making a difference	Professionalism	Structure
Mastery	Prosperity	Success
Mellowness	Reason	Support
Meticulousness	Reasonableness	Sympathy
Mindfulness	Recognition	Synergy
Modesty	Relaxation	Teamwork
Motivation	Reliability	Thoroughness
Obedience	Religiousness	Traditionalism
Open-mindedness	Resilience	Trust
Optimism	Resourcefulness	Truth

Understanding	Usefulness	Wealth
Uniqueness	Variety	Wisdom
Unity	Vision	Zeal

Create a Prioritized List of Your Values

Now I'm going to ask you to do something that will probably feel difficult, so brace yourself. I want you to put the values you've just identified in order of priority. This may seem especially challenging because it will force you to choose one value over another, when it may feel like all of the values are equally important to you.

Keep in mind that even though I'm asking you to put your values in order of their importance, I'm not asking you to actually *throw away* one value at the expense of another, but rather to prioritize them. Having a prioritized list—one that you can use to guide your career planning and choices—makes decisions much easier for Career Cowards later.

Grab your list of your top 10 to 20 values and here we go…

1. If you have more than 10 values on your list, begin by choosing the 10 that are most important to you. Be on the lookout for any values on your list that are very similar, such as "wealth" and "prosperity" and could be combined.

1. _____
2. _____
3. _____
4. _____
5. _____
6. _____
7. _____

8. _____

9. _____

10. _____

2. Now imagine that you are on a road trip with a group of people who are especially important in your life. You are all traveling cross-country, in a comfortable motor home, to an important event that you don't want to miss. Right now you are crossing a stretch of desert that continues on for more than 1,000 miles with very few gas stations along the way. This leg of the trip will take you three days to complete. But your vehicle is gassed up and well stocked, so you don't anticipate any problems.

    Unfortunately though, the air-conditioning in the motor home stops working shortly after you begin driving through the desert. It's hot and you want your traveling partners to be comfortable. At one of the few available gas stations, the mechanic says he will fix your air-conditioning in exchange for one of your top 10 values. You decide to give him this one:

    Value #10 _____

3. You continue on your way, now comfortably cooled by a functioning air conditioner. But you realize that when you stopped at the gas station, a rattlesnake slithered into your motor home and is now threatening to strike. You have the power to make the rattlesnake disappear by giving up another value. You choose to give away…

    Value #9 _____

4. Making further progress through the desert, it is now time for lunch. You open the refrigerator and cupboards to fix your friends a meal, and discover that the food you purchased to be loaded into the motor home was forgotten. You could probably survive for three days without food, but one of your travel mates is diabetic and needs a steady supply of nourishment.

Just then you pass a lunch wagon. You flag him down and decide to purchase three days' worth of food in exchange for this value:

Value #8 _____

5. You and your friends are now cool and fed, making your way across the desert. Then you notice a woman waving a white rag on the road ahead, pleading for you to stop. She explains that her car stopped running several miles down the road and she is stranded. You agree to take her aboard your motor home, at the expense of this value:

Value #7 _____

6. Happy to be moving again (despite all of these interruptions) you, your friends, and your new traveler become better acquainted. Then one of your friends receives a call on his cell phone, telling him that his daughter needs emergency surgery, and they need him back home as soon as possible. You are able to arrange a helicopter to rendezvous with you in the desert and deliver him safely to his daughter's hospital, by trading in this value:

Value #6 _____

7. You wave goodbye to your friend and begin your trip once more. No further catastrophes stop you on this day, and eventually you pull off the road to sleep for the night. In the morning, however, you discover that the back end of the motor home has begun to sink into a pit of quicksand, and the only way to get it out is by giving up this value:

Value #5 _____

8. Back on the road, you begin the trip once again. During the night, however, a deadly spider crept into the motor home and bit one of your friends. He is struggling to breathe. You contact

emergency services and they describe a plant that you can easily find in the desert as an antidote, in exchange for this value:

Value #4 _____

9. Thankfully, the antidote worked and your friend is now fine. But then you discover that the spider not only bit your friend, he also bit a hole in your cistern, and all of your drinking water has drained away. You still have two more days in the desert, and you must find water. At another of the rare gas stations along the way, you trade this value for a new, fully filled cistern of water:

   Value #3 _____

10. The rest of Day #2 on the desert road is uneventful, thankfully. You have water, food, and healthy passengers, and you're making great time. Again, you stop to sleep for the night. But during the night, a crazed killer, escaped from a nearby prison, has kidnapped one of your passengers. You can secure her safe return in exchange for this value:

    Value #2 _____

11. Your friend safely back with the group, you *finally* exit the desert, with this one last value still in your possession:

    Value #1 _____

Well done! You've just completed prioritizing your values list. Hang onto this valuable tool. Not only will it help you execute a smooth career change, it can also help you with other significant decisions in your life.

Why It's Worth Doing

Remember a time when you struggled to make a decision? Or a circumstance when you rushed into a choice without adequately thinking things through and then later regretted your actions? Most likely, the frustration you felt in a situation like one of these involved a values conflict—one of those times when a choice you made clashed with something else that was more important to you.

For example, I was once offered a well-paying contract to perform some career counseling services that I would have *loved* to do. Yet something was holding me back from accepting the contract. "Why am I not jumping on this?" I kept asking myself. For two days I wrestled with myself, feeling paralyzed. Then I decided to practice what I preach: I pulled out my prioritized list of values. The number-one value on my list is "family," and I aim to maintain a smooth-running life for myself, my husband, and my children.

Right then, I could see why I hadn't accepted the contract immediately. Part of the contract would require me to travel for an extended period of time, leaving my family behind. Accepting the contract would have meant compromising my "family" value. Suddenly, it was clear what I needed to do: Unless I could negotiate a shorter travel period, I would have to let the opportunity go. In the end, I was able to talk the employer into less travel, and my values conflict was resolved.

Having a defined, prioritized list of values helps you remain faithful to yourself, especially during stressful times (such as when you're trying to choose between one exciting career opportunity and another). Not having a clear list of values to refer to is like being lost without a compass.

Career Champ Profile: Terrance

Terrance was struggling to define a career plan for himself. He'd already done many things in an attempt to create a satisfying career: He'd completed a bachelor's degree in economics as well as an MBA, and had taken several skill-building courses and workshops. He'd read several career planning books and researched numerous career options using information he'd located on the Internet, yet still he felt confused and frustrated.

"Complete this visualization exercise," I suggested. He looked at me skeptically. I could guess that he was thinking, "*Another* career exercise…I've already done so many, and none of them has helped!" But I nagged him to at least give it a try. Reluctantly, he agreed.

Terrance and I met a week later. He walked into my office with a look of joy on his face. "This was great!" he began. "It allowed me to look at my potential career path from the top down, rather than from ground level. I was able to see things much more clearly this way!"

In completing the visualization exercise, Terrance had seen a picture for himself that had him living and working in three places in the world—New York City, Africa, and his hometown in Colorado—at different times during the year. In each place he handled different tasks. In Colorado, for instance, he saw himself doing most of his planning work for a nonprofit agency aiming to reduce poverty in the world. In New York, he pictured himself networking with major donors who could fund the nonprofit's efforts. And in Africa, he visualized himself overseeing the implementation of his planning and fund-raising efforts.

After analyzing and prioritizing the values in his visualization, Terrance came up with this list:

1. Education

2. Helpfulness

3. Family

4. Security

5. Proactivity

6. Organization

7. Leadership

8. Abundance

9. Teamwork

10. Honesty

"Until I completed this exercise, I hadn't been able to see how my talents and interests could be combined into a career opportunity that would support my priorities in life. But now it's all pretty clear!" he said.

Core Courage Concept

Putting your values on paper takes guts. It forces you to say, "In my life, *this* is more important than *that*." It can almost seem easier to blindly move through life, avoiding the decisions that really cause us to sweat. Yet the downside to this approach is that although we may sidestep the challenge of a tough decision, we also miss out on the opportunity to choose what is *truly* right for us—and make decisions that will ultimately make us much happier in life.

Confidence Checklist

☐ Create a picture of your ideal work and life.

☐ Uncover the values hidden in your ideal situation.

☐ Create a prioritized list of your values.

Chapter 3

Pinpoint Your Passion Zones

Excited about the strengths, talents, and values you've identified so far? Keep the momentum going by tapping into your passion zones—specific industries that exist in the world of work that will be especially interesting and meaningful to you. This is a critical (and fun) step toward achieving your career-change goals.

Risk It or Run From It?

- **Risk Rating:** Zilch. (Your most taxing challenges will be using a highlighter and looking up some things on the Internet.)

- **Payoff Potential:** Huge beyond words! This single chapter can help you crack the code for finding career options that inspire and satisfy you.

- **Time to Complete:** 30 minutes to a few hours, depending on how much fun you want to have.

- **Bailout Strategy:** Skipping this step will leave a gaping hole in your career-change process. At the minimum, look through the industries list and highlight 20 that you love.

(continued)

(continued)

> - **The "20 Percent Extra" Edge:** Having a defined list of your passion zones provides you with a wealth of possibilities for finding, and maintaining, career satisfaction. Most people are clueless about their passion zones. Complete the following steps and you'll be much more in tune with what's truly motivating and meaningful to you.
>
> - **"Go For It!" Bonus Activity:** When you get to the passion zone–combining step, call together a group of three or more people you trust and ask them to help you brainstorm ideas.

How to Create a List of Your Most Motivating Passion Zones

"Passion"…such a loaded word! People typically associate passion with excitement, sex, and sometimes even a crazed fanaticism. In terms of your career, however, I'll be referring to passions — or "passion zones" — as those interest areas that are especially meaningful or intriguing to you.

For instance, one of my passion zones is yoga. I *love* doing it, I love how good it is for me, and I'm willing to endure hour after hour of intense physical effort to learn more about it and to become more skilled. A few of my other passion zones are cooking, reading, career counseling, knitting, rollerblading, professional development, and volunteering.

There are thousands of passion zones, and each person's passion zone preferences are unique. In terms of career planning, your unique passion zones can point you in directions that will lead to long-term career satisfaction and success. The following activities will show you how to identify your passion zones for use in your career-change process.

Identify Several of Your Unique Passion Zones

A first step toward identifying your passion zones is to create a long list of those that are appealing to you. Following is a listing of hundreds of passion zone topics. Look over the list and then complete the exercises that follow.

Accounting

- Bookkeeping
- Consulting
- Payroll Services
- Tax Preparation

Advertising

- Agency
- Art & Layout
- Commercial
- Computer
- Copywriting
- Desktop Publishing
- Displays
- Media Buyers
- Online
- Outdoor
- Radio, Television

Aging

- Alzheimer's
- Human Services Organizations
- Osteoporosis
- Senior Citizens Organizations

Agriculture

- Chemicals
- Consulting
- Crop Farming
- Fish Farming
- Greenhouses
- Livestock Farming
- Nursery
- Orchards
- Products & Services

Aircraft
- Airports
- Charters
- Gliders
- Helicopters
- Rentals & Leases
- Schools

Animals
- Aid and Welfare
- Boarding
- Cemeteries
- Dealers, Pet Shops
- Humane Societies, Shelters
- Pet Adoption
- Pet Sitting
- Products & Services
- Rescue
- Training
- Veterinary Medicine
- Veterinary Schools

Architecture
- Commercial
- Computer-Assisted Design (CAD)
- Consulting
- Design Services
- Engineering Services
- Firms
- Industrial Design
- Landscape Architecture

Arts
- Craft Stores
- Fiber Arts
- Galleries
- Museums
- Music Groups

- Painting
- Performing Arts
- Restoration & Conservation
- Sculpting
- Supplies & Equipment
- Theatre Companies
- Theatres

Automobiles & Trucks

- Collision Repair
- Commercial Vehicle Leasing
- Dealerships
- Renting & Leasing

Business & Professional Services

- Administrative
- Business Service Centers
- Credit Bureau
- Document Storage Services
- Editing
- Mail Centers
- Messenger Service
- Office Equipment
- Office Supplies

Chemical

- Industrial
- Manufacturing
- Organic
- Petroleum
- Synthetic

Clothing

- Accessories
- Alterations
- Apparel Manufacturing
- Children's
- Leather Products & Services
- Men's

- Retail
- Shoe Manufacturing
- Shoe Stores
- Women's

Community Organizations

- Child & Family Services
- Day Care Services
- Elderly Residential Care
- Emergency & Relief Services
- Housing Programs
- Services for those with Disabilities
- Shelters
- Social Assistance
- Urban & Rural Planning & Development

Computers

- Computer-Assisted Design (CAD)
- Consulting
- Data Recovery
- DSL
- Hardware
- Installation
- Internet Access
- Networking
- Products & Services
- Schools
- Security
- Service & Repair
- Software
- Software Publishers
- Training

Construction

- Developing
- Equipment
- Highway, Street, Bridge, & Tunnel
- Manufactured Homes & Buildings

- Plumbing, Heating, & Air Conditioning
- Power & Communication Transmission Lines
- Products & Services
- Remodeling
- Residential & Commercial
- Surveying
- Water, Sewer, & Pipeline

Contractors
- Carpentry
- Electrical
- Excavating
- Painting
- Roofing
- Special Trades
- Well Drilling

Courier Services

Deaf Services

Education
- Administration
- Colleges & Universities
- Community College/Junior College
- Developmental Delays
- Elementary School
- Exam Preparation
- High School
- Middle School
- Parochial
- Private
- Public
- Special Education
- Technical & Trade Schools
- Vocational Schools

Employment
- Agencies
- Career Counseling

- Employee Leasing
- Executive Search Firms
- Job Placement Firms
- Resume Services
- Temporary

Engineering

- Acoustical
- Civil
- Communication
- Consulting
- Electrical
- Electronic
- Environmental
- Forensic
- Foundation
- Geotechnical—Soils
- Logging
- Manufacturing
- Mechanical
- Mining
- Refrigeration
- Research & Development
- Sanitary
- Structural
- Traffic/Transportation
- Water Supply

Environment

- Consulting
- GPS/GIS
- Renewable Resources

Events

- Auditoriums
- Banquets
- Booking Agencies
- Conference Centers

- Conventions, Symposiums
- Party Planning Services
- Stadiums
- Wedding Planning Services

Family Services

- Abuse
- Adoption Services
- Child Protection Services
- Crisis Intervention
- Dependency & Neglect
- Domestic Violence
- Family Planning
- Human Services Organizations
- Pregnancy
- Sexual Abuse
- Social Service Agencies

Finance

- Bank
- Collection Agencies
- Commercial Bank
- Consumer Lending
- Credit Card Issuing
- Credit Unions
- Funds, Trusts, & Estates
- International Trade Financing
- Investments
- Mortgage Lending
- Pensions
- Portfolio Management
- Savings & Loan
- Savings Institutions
- Securities
- Trading

Fire

- Alarm Systems

- Departments
- Extinguishers, Sprinklers
- Firewood
- Hydrants
- Investigations
- Safety Engineering
- Smoke & Damage Repair & Cleaning

Food & Beverage
- Bakeries
- Bars
- Beer, Wine, & Liquor Stores
- Catering Products & Services
- Coffee & Tea Manufacturing
- Cooking Schools
- Dairy Products
- Fast Food
- Food Manufacturing
- Frozen Foods
- Grocery Stores
- Microbrewing
- Personal Chefs
- Restaurant Products & Services
- Restaurants
- Seafood

Forestry
- Conservation
- Reclamation
- Timber & Logging

Garden
- Bonsai
- Florists
- Greenhouses
- Home & Garden Stores
- Landscaping Services
- Lawnmower Services

- Nurseries
- Products & Services
- Sprinklers

Government Organizations

- Federal Government
- Inspection Agencies
- International Affairs
- Labor Unions
- Licensing Agencies
- Local Government
- National Security
- State Government

Home Products & Services

- Appliances
- Automation
- Carpets
- Cleaning Services
- Furniture
- Security
- Window Treatments

Hunting

- Trapping
- Fishing
- Licenses

Industrial Supplies & Services

Insurance

- Agencies
- Business
- Commercial
- Health
- Homeowner's
- Liability
- Life
- Medical
- Personal

Invention Services

Investigating

- Detective Agencies
- Police Departments
- Private Investigating

Legal

- Attorneys
- Courts
- Law Schools
- Legal Aid
- Paralegal Support

Manufacturing & Production

- Aluminum, Copper
- Appliances & Housewares
- Architectural Products
- Cement & Concrete Products
- Commercial & Industrial Product
- Computer & Electronic Equipment
- Electrical Equipment
- Engines
- Fabricated Metals Products
- Fertilizer
- Home Products
- Instruments
- Iron & Steel
- Machine Shops
- Machinery
- Metals
- Paints & Coatings
- Paper
- Pharmaceuticals
- Plastic & Rubber Products
- Soaps & Cleaning Compounds
- Sporting & Athletic Goods
- Vehicle

Medical & Health Care

- Acupuncture
- Addictions/Chemical Dependency
- AIDS Research
- Alternative Health Care
- Blood Banks
- Dentistry
- Eating Disorders
- Eyeglasses
- Family Planning
- Health Care Products
- HMOs
- Homeopathy
- Internal Medicine
- Medical & Diagnostic Laboratories
- Mental Health
- Naturopathy
- Nursing
- Occupational Therapy
- Opticians
- Organ Donation
- Personal Care Products
- Pharmacies & Drugstores
- Physicians
- Psychiatry
- Psychology
- Public Health
- Speech Therapy
- Stress Reduction
- Surgeons
- Weight Maintenance & Reduction

Military

- Draft
- Recruiting Offices
- Veteran's Affairs

Mining & Drilling
- Oil & Gas Extraction
- Coal
- Metals
- Products & Services

Moving Services
- Mini-Warehouses & Self Storage Units
- Moving Companies
- Van & Truck Rental

Personal Services & Care
- Beauty Salons
- Day Spas
- Hair Salons
- Massage Therapy
- Nail Salons
- Spas

Pets
- Clinics
- Hospitals
- Stores
- Veterinary Care

Photography
- Aerial
- Commercial
- Fine Art
- Galleries
- Photo Finishing
- Portrait
- Schools
- Supplies & Equipment

Physical Fitness
- Classes
- Clothing
- Equipment

- Gyms
- Personal Training
- Pilates
- Schools
- Shoes
- Yoga

Printing & Publishing

- Book Binding
- Book Restoration & Conservation
- Books
- Commercial
- Desktop
- Digital
- Libraries
- Magazines
- Newsstands
- Periodicals
- Prepress Services
- Support, Products, & Services

Public Safety

- Fire Protection
- Police Academy
- Police Agencies
- Sheriff's Office

Public Utilities

Real Estate

- Agents & Brokers
- Appraising
- Commercial Property Management
- Inspections
- Rental & Leasing
- Residential Property Management
- Warehouses

Recreation

- Amusement Parks

- Boats
- Gambling Industries
- Golf Courses
- Parks
- Shooting Ranges
- Skate Parks
- Skiing/Snowboarding
- Theme Parks

Religious Organizations

- Churches
- Convents
- Monasteries
- Religious Counseling
- Spiritual Counseling

Research Services

- Design
- Education
- Environmental
- Laboratory
- Legal
- Marketing
- Medical
- Product

Retail

- Bookstore Cafes
- Bookstores
- Boutiques
- Clothing
- Department Stores
- Jewelry
- Malls
- Outlets
- Shoes
- Specialty Stores

Safety Consulting
- Accident Reconstruction

Shopping Services

Space Research & Technology

Sports
- Clubs
- Equipment
- Gyms
- Lessons
- Professional Sports Teams
- Racetracks
- Team Apparel
- Teams

Telecommunications & Broadcasting
- Cable Networks
- Call Centers
- Equipment
- Installation & Repair
- Radio Networks
- Radio Stations
- Satellite Communications
- Systems
- Television Networks
- Television Production
- Television Stations
- Wired Communication
- Wireless Communication

Teleproduction
- Video Production Companies

Textiles
- Fabric Stores
- Fiber, Yarn, & Thread Mills
- Rug & Carpet Mills
- Spinning Equipment & Services

Tourism

- Art Galleries
- Attractions
- Bicycle Tours
- Boat Renting & Leasing
- Campgrounds
- Chambers of Commerce
- Cruises
- Guest Ranches
- Guide Services
- Historic Places & Services
- Hunting & Fishing Preserves
- Parks
- Racetracks
- Recreation Centers
- Resorts
- River Trips
- Zoos

Transportation

- Airlines
- Airports
- Auto & Diesel Repair
- Bus Service
- Cargo Transport
- Freight Trucking
- Gas & Oil Pipelines
- Local Rail Transit
- School Bus Companies
- Ships — Cargo
- Taxi Companies
- Trains — Cargo
- Trains — Passenger

Travel

- Accommodations
- Agencies

- Airline Reservations
- Bus Tours
- Cruises
- Package Tours
- RVs
- Scenic Tours

Utilities

- Electric Power
- Hydroelectric Power
- Natural Gas Power
- Nuclear Power
- Wind Power

Vehicles

- ATVs
- Cars
- Motorcycles
- RVs
- Trailers
- Trucks

Waste

- Collection
- Management
- Recycling
- Treatment & Disposal

Wholesale

- Apparel
- Commercial Products
- Construction Products
- Drugs & Druggist's Products
- Electrical Goods
- Electronic Goods
- Food
- Footwear
- Home Furnishings & Products
- Lumber

- Paper & Paper Products
- Petroleum Products
- Recreational Products & Vehicles
- Vehicles

Wood

- Engineered Products
- Millwork
- Preservation
- Products
- Sawmills

Review the list of passion zones and highlight, check, or underline as many of them as seem interesting to you. If you have even the smallest glimmer of attraction or fascination with a particular topic (but haven't yet experienced it firsthand), mark it anyway. Salsa Dancing, for instance, is a topic that interests me even though I've never really done it. Also feel free to look through the Yellow Pages section in your phone book. It identifies even more categories.

Panic Point! At this stage in the process, most people automatically begin to limit or "edit" their choices. For example, let's say that you see the topic "Private Investigations" and you think, "Sure, that topic interests me. I'd like the idea of digging up dirt on people's backgrounds, especially if it helps uncover bad guys before they get into any more trouble. But in reality I have *no* experience or training with private investigations. Be real; what are the chances that I'd ever *really* have the chance to get involved in that kind of area? Better not check that one...." If this is how you're thinking, I encourage you to Whoa, Nellie! At this stage in the career-change process, your aim is to develop a list of as many topics as you can that seem appealing to you. *You will have the chance to edit (and make practical decisions) about your choices later, I promise!* But for now, please allow yourself to highlight every topic that intrigues you. By permitting yourself to choose a long list of interesting topics *now*, you greatly increase your chances for uncovering many more excellent-fit career opportunities later.

When your Practical Self jumps in with, "Be practical! Don't check that one!" tell him or her, "While I appreciate your interest in protecting me, for now, I'm going to have a little fun and choose things that seem exciting to me, even if they seem a little unrealistic. I promise that in the near future, I'll be calling on you for your good judgment once again."

Now, back to the highlighting. I encourage you to choose a *minimum* of 30 passion zone topics from the list. Here are a few tips to help in your selections:

- **Avoid thinking in terms of "job titles," and instead look at the topics as "industry categories."** *This is an extremely important point.* Often, people look at the passion zone list and immediately think, "I need to find *job titles* in here that interest me." Warning! Warning! For this exercise, *we're not focusing on job titles*. Instead, we're paying attention to industry categories.

  By considering entire passion zone industries—rather than specific job titles—you open yourself up to many more possibilities for yourself. For example, the topic "Hotels" is an industry category where an entire world of activities exists: people building hotel units, marketing hotel services, checking in guests, cooking food for them, cleaning their rooms, organizing their events, maintaining the hotel grounds, processing their expenses, and so on. Within the hotel industry, there may be several possible specialties that fit your talents, skills, and interests. By focusing on broader passion zone industries now, you allow yourself the opportunity to identify many more great-fit career-change possibilities later. To further paint a picture of passion zone industries versus specific job titles, here are a few more examples:

"Passion Zone" Industry Categories (you want to focus on this column...)	Sample Job Titles Within that Industry (...and ignore this column for now)
Travel	Flight attendant, writer of travel articles, travel planner, hotel owner, taxi driver, chef...
Web Sites	Designer, programmer, salesperson, research analyst, accountant...
Security Systems	Installer, business owner, developer, dispatcher, law enforcer...
Banks	Teller, credit analyst, personal banker, manager, loan officer...
Furniture	Designer, manufacturer, salesperson, refinisher, upholsterer, store owner...

- **Imagine that you have a Passion Zone Tour Genie.** He is going to make it possible for you to spend 15 minutes experiencing every passion zone you choose, guaranteeing that you will feel no pain and risk no loss during your visit. With this opportunity to take a risk-free tour of several passion zones, which topics will you choose?

- **Make believe that you will live for 200 years.** During this time on earth, you may become involved with many things. Your long life allows you to experience these interests with no pain or loss to you. In which areas will you spend your centuries?

- **Envision yourself as a superhuman with the power to succeed with *anything* you attempt.** Knowing that it's impossible for you to fail, which passion zones might you choose to explore?

- Pretend that you'll be given $1 million simply for choosing 5 to 10 passion zones that, although they seem interesting to you, are out of character with what you've pursued or experienced so far in your life. Which 5 to 10 "wild hare" industries would you choose?

By now you should have identified 30 or more passion zones that are appealing to you. List them here:

My Passion Zone List

_____   _____

_____   _____

_____   _____

_____   _____

_____   _____

_____   _____

_____   _____

_____   _____

_____   _____

_____   _____

_____   _____

_____   _____

_____   _____

Make Your Passion Zone Ideas Even More Appealing

Think of one of your favorite dishes. For me, it's a raspberry tart. Now think about the ingredients that go into your favorite dish. My raspberry tart is created with a crisp, buttery-sugary crust and moist, tangy berries. Yum! And while I enjoy the buttery-sugary crust all by itself, as well as like eating plain raspberries, when I put those two ingredients together, the result is something that I love much, much more!

With this idea in mind—the concept of combining two (or more) things that you like, resulting in something that you love even more—we're going to have some fun with the passion zones you selected in the preceding step.

Look at your list of passion zones and choose two, just to get started. Ideally it works best to choose two passion zones that don't naturally "go" together. For instance, "Gardening" and "Landscaping" seem pretty similar, so instead of choosing those two, consider choosing "Gardening" and "Computers," which don't seem as naturally aligned. Write your two passion zone topics here:

Passion Zone Topic #1 _____

Passion Zone Topic #2 _____

Panic Point! As a Career Coward, you may be thinking, "Oh no! Which two do I choose? I don't want to choose the wrong ones!" Keep in mind that for now, we're just experimenting and having fun. No matter what you choose for this experiment, it will be okay. And in just a little while, you'll have the chance to choose more topics. In fact, you can choose as many topics as you want, so don't worry about choosing the "wrong" ones.

Now, just as I like to combine a buttery-sugary crust with plain raspberries, you're going to combine your two topics to come up with something different…that you may like even better! I call these new, combined topics *blended passion zones.*

A reminder: As you go through this process, you'll once again be considering *industry topics* rather than job titles. So if you catch yourself thinking, "Hmmm, would I like a job that involves *X*," STOP and redirect your thinking to, "Hmmm, does topic *X* seem at all appealing to me?"

You can identify blended passion zones in a variety of ways. As you come up with these new ideas, write down any that seem interesting to you.

1. **Blend passion zones using a search engine:** Log onto your favorite search engine Web site (such as Google), type in two of your passion zone topics, and click the Search button. For example, when I typed in Gardening and Computers, Google.com produced 17 million references (yes, *17 million!*). I looked at the first 50 (of which many were useless), and I was able to uncover the following blended topics worth writing down:

   - Garden shopping online
   - Gardening software
   - Gardening Web sites
   - Recycling computers
   - Online gardening courses
   - Gardening blogs
   - Radio talk shows about gardening accessed through your computer

   And if I'd wanted to, I could have spent additional time looking through the other 16,999,950 Google items for even more ideas!

2. **Brainstorming "company mergers":** Pretend that you own two companies, one that deals with Passion Zone Topic #1 (in

this example, Gardening) and another that deals with Passion Zone Topic #2 (Computers). Now imagine that you're going to merge these two companies together. Ask yourself, "What new products or services will this merged company produce?" For instance, I came up with the following company merger ideas:

- Gardening equipment with computer-based controls

- Computer systems that monitor gardens (for moisture, temperature, nutrients, etc.)

- Hand-held computer tools that you can carry around with you in the garden for planning and problem-solving purposes

- Automated sprinkler systems

- Outdoor yard-monitoring security systems

Aim to brainstorm at least five new product and service ideas for each company merger combination.

3. **Have an idea party.** Bring together three or more people and ask them to brainstorm blended-industry ideas from your list of 30+ passion zones. Based on experience, it seems to work best to present your group with two or three topics at a time and ask them to offer ideas about how these passion zone industries could be blended to create a different industry. To keep the ideas flowing successfully, never pooh-pooh an idea, even if you think it's a lousy one. Write down *every* idea offered. If you feel the need to comment on a suggestion, say, "Hmm…interesting." This remark works well regardless of whether you think an idea is a good one or bad one.

Compile a Long List of Your Passion Zone Topics

Once you've finished blending two passion zone topics, choose two more, and two more, and so on, until you've experimented with several combinations. It's fine to use passion zone topics more than once, blending them with different passion zones to achieve new results. Also consider blending three or more passion zone topics at once to identify other ideas.

Your goal is to develop at least 20 new blended passion zone ideas. You'll add those to your original 30+ passion zone choices, resulting in a long list of 50+ passion zones. As with your Top Skills and Talents and Values List, prepare your passion zones list and set it aside for use in a future chapter.

Blended Passion Zones List

Why It's Worth Doing

When I was studying career counseling in graduate school, I took a class called "Tests and Assessments." It reviewed several of the most popular career assessments available—you know what I mean, those fill-in-the-bubbles questionnaires that when completed tell you that you'd probably love being a toilet scrubber.

Well, I'm exaggerating a little; I don't think "toilet scrubber" is on the list of job titles. But for the vast majority of people I've surveyed about their experiences with those types of career assessments, most have been very disappointed with the results. "I have no interest in being a (you fill in the blank...bus driver, teacher, physicist, bean counter...)."

"What's going on?" I began to wonder. "Why are the results of these assessments so off base?" Researchers devoted significant time and resources to creating quality tools, yet they were failing!

The answer came to me one day as I sat in on a lecture presented by career gurus Dr. Richard Bolles and Daniel Porot. Porot was talking about using the Yellow Pages as a tool to help career counseling clients identify industries of interest. Just then, I had a huge "Ah-ha!" moment. I realized that simply possessing a talent or skill isn't enough. To gain satisfaction from that strength, we must *use it in a way that is meaningful to us.*

Most career assessments focus on identifying the *skills* we like to use, but they don't help us identify meaningful ways in which to use them. For example, you may discover that you have a talent for calculating numbers, and a career assessment may tell you, "You'd be a great accountant." "That sounds kinda boring," you might think. Yet what if one of your passion zones is conserving the environment, and the results had said, "You'd probably like managing the finances for an organization involved in conserving our environment"? Your reaction would probably have been, "Cool! Bring it on!"

Identifying passion zones gives you a way to build excitement and significance into your career-change process, providing you with starting points for finding career options that are especially interesting and meaningful to you.

Career Champ Profile: Eileen

Eileen worked as a receptionist at a doctor's office. Although she disliked her tasks—answering phones, scheduling patients, and keeping the magazines neatly stacked in the waiting room—she loved the science side of what was going on behind the scenes. The idea of analyzing scientific information to come up with an answer to a problem was fascinating to her.

When researching options for her career change, Eileen selected testing labs, biology, and science-related industries as a few of her passion zones. When she blended these interests, she was able to identify several additional intriguing ideas. One that really stood out to her was Forensic Laboratories, where specialists analyze evidence to help solve crimes. "That seems so cool!" she said, her eyes shining at the possibility of somehow getting involved with a forensic lab environment.

A few days later, still very excited about the idea, Eileen took a tour of a government-run forensic lab located near her home. On her tour, she was able to learn about many specialties within a forensic lab environment. The position that seemed most intriguing to her was the job of a scientist studying evidence at a lab bench. To learn more about this role, Eileen interviewed a few forensic scientists about their work. What they described about their specialty caused Eileen to become even more excited. Eileen set her sights on switching careers from medical office receptionist to forensic scientist.

Over the next few months, Eileen landed a job as an assistant at the lab. Although it was a low-level position, it was a start. Over time, Eileen earned a doctorate in forensic science. Now, instead of straightening magazines, Eileen works at a lab bench, helping to straighten out the mysteries of crimes.

Core Courage Concept

It can be scary to admit to yourself that something excites and inspires you. To say, "I'm really jazzed about the idea of *X*" (you fill in the blank) is a little like baring your soul. What if you admit your interest, but then find out that it's impossible for you to achieve?

That *is* an overwhelming thought…to identify an area you're passionate about, and not to be able to achieve it. Yet remember this: There are literally *millions* of career specialties in our world today, and that number just keeps growing. Within those millions of career specialties, there are *hundreds* of options that could provide you with meaning and the career satisfaction you seek (you just need to identify them, and that's what you're working on right now). And of those hundreds, there will be *several* opportunities that you will be able to realistically achieve — I promise!

By simply allowing yourself to identify your passion zones through this chapter's easy and fun exercises, you're taking a huge step toward identifying several of those great-fit, realistic, "I can make this happen!" career-change opportunities that exist for you.

Confidence Checklist

- ☐ Identify several of your unique passion zones.
- ☐ Make your passion zone ideas even more appealing.
- ☐ Compile a long list of your passion zone topics.

Part 2

Exploring New Career Ideas

Chapter 4

Create a List of Career Ideas That Jazz You

Been searching for great-fit career ideas that make the most of your talents, skills, and interests? You'll find them in this chapter! Here's the chance to combine your strengths with topics that are important and meaningful for you, resulting in several terrific, customized career options.

Risk It or Run From It?

- **Risk Rating:** Low to none at all (it's about as much of a hazard as trying on several different outfits from clothes in your closet).

- **Payoff Potential:** Colossal! This is where we combine things you love—talents and skills you possess, with passions that get your blood pumping—into concrete career ideas that can skyrocket you into the career-satisfaction stratosphere!

- **Time to Complete:** 30 to 60 minutes.

- **Bailout Strategy:** For something this fun and easy, with such a huge payoff, I wouldn't recommend skipping it—even if you think you know exactly where your career change is

(continued)

(continued)

headed. But if you must (sigh), at least write down three specific career-change targets that interest you, made up of both the career role you'd like to have and the industry you'd like to work in.

- **The "20 Percent Extra" Edge:** Matching roles that capitalize on your strengths with passion zones that intrigue you is a process so powerful it can launch your career-change goals from, "I'd like to wind up in something that's at least a little better than what I'm doing now," to "I could create something really fantastic for myself!" This process will provide you with a goldmine of terrific possibilities, and inspire you to accomplish great things in your career.

- **"Go For It!" Bonus Activity:** After you've completed the Career-Choices Compass exercise, choose additional job titles and industries from your lists and complete the compass again, to come up with even more great ideas.

How to Identify Several Great-Fit Career-Change Opportunities

Much of the hard work you've done so far will now be put to good use. You'll be able to combine your Top Skills and Talents (from chapter 1) and Passion Zones (from chapter 3) lists (we'll use the Values List from chapter 2 later)—to identify several exciting career opportunities that fit your unique strengths and interests.

Put Your Skills and Talents to Work

You identified your best skills and talents in chapter 1. Now you're going to transform those unique strengths into potential job titles. Be prepared—this process is so simple, it almost seems too easy!

Here's how it works: Take your strengths from your list of Top Skills and Talents, and turn each one into a role or job title, simply by changing the ending or moving the words around a little. Often all it takes is adding "er," "or," or "ist" to the skill or talent (whichever one makes more sense), for example

- "Calculating data" becomes "Data Calculator."

- "Delegating" becomes "Delegator."

- "Disseminating Information" becomes "Information Disseminator."

- "Encouraging others" becomes "Encourager."

- "Helping others" becomes "Helper."

- "Managing conflict" becomes "Conflict Manager."

- "Proposing ideas" becomes "Idea Proposer."

- "Writing" becomes "Writer."

See...pretty simple (even Career Cowards usually don't sweat with this one!). And while some of the titles may seem a little different from the traditional titles you see in a job ad (for instance, "Idea Proposer" isn't an ordinary job title), you'll still probably get the gist of what that role would entail. So right now, turn your Top Skills and Talents into titles and write them here. Aim to create a list of at least 10, and up to 20, titles.

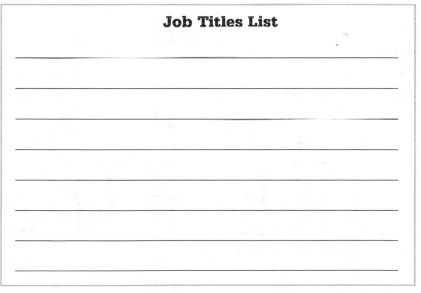

Job Titles List

(continued)

(continued)

_____

_____

_____

_____

_____

_____

_____

Tip: When in doubt, the titles "specialist," "coordinator," and "project manager" are good choices.

With this exercise, you'll sometimes run into skills or talents that don't easily convert over into logical job titles. You can usually work around this problem as Brad did by asking yourself, "In what job role(s) might I be using this skill?" and then writing down those titles instead.

Panic Point! Have you run into a skill or talent that doesn't easily transform itself into a title? For instance, one of my clients, Brad, had added "Intuition" to his Top Skills and Talents list. To make it a job title, he changed it to "Intuiter"—a person who would intuit things—but that didn't seem like a logical job role. So then I asked him, "In what kind of job role might you be using intuition?" "Well," he said, "as a people manager, hiring and leading them, or as an operations manager, making decisions about things." "List 'People Manager' and 'Operations Manager' as job titles instead of 'Intuiter,'" I suggested. This strategy worked well for Brad.

When you've transformed your Top Skills and Talents into job titles, choose your favorite 10—those job roles that seem to fit you best and seem most exciting to you—and write one job title inside one of each of the spaces on the Favorite Roles wheel, as is shown in the example. Tip: If two roles seem very similar, such as "Teacher" and "Trainer," feel free to combine them in a single space on the wheel.

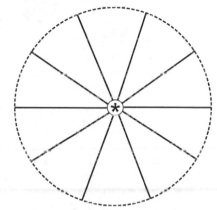

Figure 4.1: Favorite Roles wheel. On this wheel, you'll write 10 of the most appealing job titles you created in the preceding exercise. Include the roles that seem interesting and exciting to you. Have fun with it!

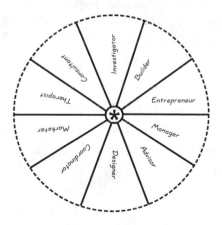

Figure 4.2: A sample completed Favorite Roles wheel. Here's an example of a filled-in wheel for William, one of my clients. There is a wide range of potential job roles that seem intriguing to him.

Select Your Most Appealing Passion Zones

Now look over your Passion Zones lists—the 50+ industries you selected from both the Industries List (on page 61) and the Blended Passion Zones exercise (on page 65)—and choose the 20 that are most interesting and appealing to you at this moment.

Panic Point! When asked to pick their 20 most appealing passion zones, most Career Cowards will experience anxiety that might feel something like this: "Although I find the topic of 'Movie Production' *appealing,* my Practical Self is telling me 'Really, what are the chances that *you* are going to actually get involved in movie production? What's the sense in even choosing it?'" You probably remember having a similar battle with your Practical Self in chapter 3, when you were selecting your passion zones in the first place. And at that time I recommended telling your Practical Self, "While I appreciate your interest in protecting me, for now, I'm going to have a little fun and choose things that seem exciting to me, even if they seem a little unrealistic. I promise that in the near future, I'll be calling on you for your good judgment once again." This same advice applies here. For now your aim is to choose things that are *especially appealing and motivating to you.* We will allow your Practical Self to have final decision-making power about your welfare later in this process, I promise! But for now, please tell him or her to take a little nap.

Once you've selected the 20 passion zones that are most appealing to you, write one in each of the spaces on the Most Appealing Passion Zones wheel, as the example shows on this wheel:

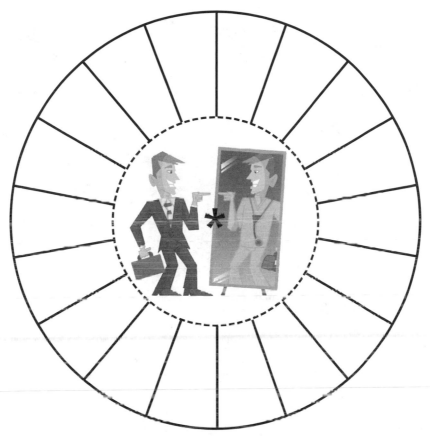

Figure 4.3: Most Appealing Passion Zones wheel. On this wheel, write 20 of your industry or "passion zone" ideas that at this moment seem most intriguing to you. Don't hold back—this is the time to explore those areas that you've always dreamed about!

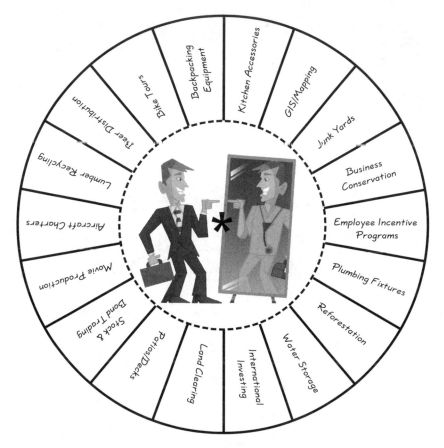

Figure 4.4: A sample completed Most Appealing Passion Zones wheel. This is William's completed Passion Zones wheel, with ideas ranging from "Stock and Bond Trading" to "Junk Yards"!

Build and Play with Your Career Choices Compass

First, you'll need to build your Career Choices Compass. Grab scissors and a paper clip, photocopy and cut out both the Favorite Roles and Most Appealing Passion Zones wheels, and place them on top of each other—with the Favorite Roles wheel inside the Most Appealing Passion Zones wheel—so that the words you've written on each wheel are visible. Next, connect the wheels with a paper clip by carefully inserting the point on the outside edge of the paper clip through the * in the center of each wheel (it may be easier to first poke a hole through each ✳ using a pin), and gently sliding the paper clip through the wheels until half of the paper clip is positioned on the top of your wheels, and half is positioned on the bottom of your wheels. The positioning of the paper clip should allow you to easily rotate the Favorite Roles wheel within the Most Appealing Passion Zones wheel. Congratulations, you've just created your Career Choices Compass—one of the most valuable tools available to you for finding true career change happiness.

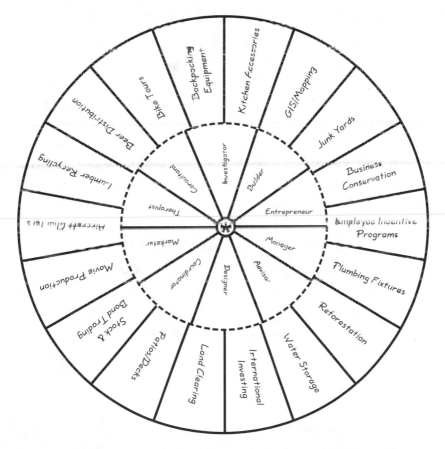

Figure 4.5: Here's an example of the two wheels combined, resulting in a motivating and useful Career Choices Compass for William. This tool provides William with 200 exciting career possibilities, from "Designer of Patios/Decks" to "Marketer of Aircraft Charters." Wow!

Now it's time to play! Go through the following steps to gain the most value from your Career Choices Compass.

1. Begin by picking any one of the titles you've written on the Favorite Roles wheel, and position it so that it's aligned with any one of the industries you've written on the Most Appealing Passion Zones wheel. (Note: It doesn't really matter which job title or industry you pick first. Eventually, you're going to work with every one of them anyway.) For example, you might pick "Writer" and position it next to "Gardening Web Site."

2. Ask yourself, "On a scale of 1 to 10, with 1 being 'Very little interest' and 10 being 'Extremely high interest,' how interesting does this particular job title-plus-industry combination seem to me?" Another way to consider the possibility is to imagine what it might be like to be involved in that particular career specialty, as in "How interesting would it be for me to write for a gardening Web site?" If this job-title-plus-industry combination seems pretty interesting to you, write it on your Career Specialties to Consider list, like this:

Career Specialties to Consider

Title	Industry
_____	_____
_____	_____
_____	_____
_____	_____
_____	_____
_____	_____
_____	_____

Title	Industry
_____	_____
_____	_____
_____	_____
_____	_____
_____	_____

3. Next, still using the first job title you chose, turn your Favorite Roles wheel one position clockwise, so that it's now aligned with the next industry on your Most Appealing Passion Zones wheel. For example, "Writer" may now be matched with "Auto Parts Catalogs." Again, ask yourself, "How interesting does this particular job-title-plus-industry combination seem to me?" And again, write any combination that seems pretty appealing to you on the Career Specialties to Consider list.

4. Continue turning your Favorite Roles wheel in a clockwise circle until you've matched your first job title with each of the 20 industries listed on your Most Appealing Passion Zones wheel. For each new combination, ask yourself the "How interesting does this combination seem to me?" question and write down every appealing match.

5. Once you've completed a full rotation of the Favorite Roles wheel using the first title you chose, move clockwise to the next job title on your Favorite Roles wheel and repeat the process, matching the new job title with the 20 industries on your Most Appealing Passion Zones wheel, considering the combinations as you go.

6. Continue this process with every job title listed on your Favorite Roles wheel, until you've matched all 10 job titles with each of the 20 industries on your Most Appealing Passion

Zones wheel. In total, you will match and rate 200 possible combinations; and ideally, you will discover at least 20 job-title-plus-industry combinations that you find pretty appealing.

Panic Point! Sometimes as Career Cowards use the Career Choices Compass to match their Favorite Roles with their Most Appealing Passion Zones, they experience these concerns: "Oh no! I'm putting these matches together, and while the combinations may seem interesting to me, *are these the only career options available?* Do my unique talents and skills and passions boil down *just to these choices?*" Or you might be thinking, "This compass thing won't work for me. I'll need to go through a much more complex process than this to identify career options that work for me." If these thoughts are crossing your mind, relax. The ideas on your Career Specialties to Consider list are just a starting point. Your unique talents, skills, and interests also fit into many *other* career options, but these are just a few to help you begin your exploration process. You'll identify more possibilities as you move through the next few steps in this book—I promise! Regarding your "This compass thing won't work for me" concern, the best advice I can offer is to give the compass your very best effort because it *does* work—even for Career Cowards!

If you're feeling panicked about creating a list of specific career-change options to consider, keep in mind that you're still in the early stages of this process. You still have a way to go before you make any final career-change decisions. Going forward, you'll have the chance to carefully research several career-change options and further refine your choices so that ultimately, you make choices that are just right for you. For now, you're just taking a small step to identify some career options to consider, without having to make any final decisions yet.

Why It's Worth Doing

Most of us are happiest when we're able to use our strengths in ways that feel meaningful and interesting to us. The process you've just completed—combining your talents and skills with your passion zones—allows you to begin to see multiple possibilities for applying what you do best to situations that you feel passionate about. And as you've probably just discovered, there aren't just one or two intriguing career-change possibilities available to you; there are *several!* You now have a wealth of options to draw from as you execute your successful career change. If you discover along the way that some of these options won't work for you for one reason or another, no problem! You still have several other great career-change possibilities from which to choose.

Career Champ Profile: Cary

Cary felt burned out in his career as a trainer at a construction engineering company. He'd fallen into his position after getting promoted from a job as an assistant on construction sites, to office manager at the company headquarters, and finally into his current role. But his job seemed boring and Cary felt stagnant in his career.

When he'd filled in his Career Choices Compass, Cary's favorite passion zones were sporting competitions, environmental nonprofit organizations, television studios, and events centers. His top job roles were trainer, organizer, and project manager. As he completed his compass at my office, he chuckled at the results. "Project manager for sporting competitions...trainer at an environmental nonprofit...organizer at a television studio...these *all* sound like so much fun!" Then he confessed to me that while the possibilities seemed exciting, his Practical Self was screaming at him, "Cary, get *real!*"

I reminded him that for now, we were just developing a list of several possibilities. He would have a chance to research his options carefully before making any major decisions. "Okay," he said, "I'll trust you on this...but I hope it works!" Over the next few months

Cary learned more about several of the areas he'd identified on his Career Specialties to Consider list. As part of his research, Cary interviewed a number of specialists about their work, including a project manager for ice-skating events at the U.S. Olympics, a program organizer for a television news station, and several people at environmental nonprofit firms. Through his interviews, Cary discovered an area he hadn't known about before, green building, an industry devoted to environmentally sound construction practices. The focus of the industry was extremely exciting to Cary, and shortly after, Cary took steps to shift from his current work into a career as a specialist in the green-building industry. Even his Practical Self was happy with his choice!

Core Courage Concept

It takes guts to admit to yourself that a career specialty seems exciting. What if you get enthused about an option, and then things don't work out? Risking that kind of disappointment is scary. Yet you *don't* want to stay stuck in what you're doing now, and you *do* want to identify a career path that makes great use of your unique talents, skills, and interests. At the very least, you owe it to yourself to push through your fears of "This exciting career area could never really happen for me," and instead tell yourself, "If a particular career idea interests me, I'm going to consider it as an option for now—because I'm worth it!"

Confidence Checklist

☐ Put your skills and talents to work.

☐ Select your most appealing passion zones.

☐ Build and play with your Career Choices Compass.

Chapter 5

Prioritize Your Top Three Choices (and Get Geared Up to Move Forward)

So here you sit, with a list of 20 or more career ideas that look pretty appealing to you (at least on paper). You may feel a little excited, and a little skeptical, too. What can you *really* do with some of these ideas? Where do you go from here? In this chapter, you'll complete a few fun, low-risk exercises that will allow you to learn more about several career areas and determine which options are worth investigating further.

Risk It or Run From It?

- **Risk Rating:** No real risk. You'll just be gathering information and making some preliminary decisions.

- **Payoff Potential:** Excellent. These steps will help you move further along your path toward career-change success.

- **Time to Complete:** One hour or more, depending on how much time you choose to put into the research activities.

- **Bailout Strategy:** If you're able to look at your Career Specialties to Consider list and pick three title-plus-industry

(continued)

(continued)

choices that you want to investigate in-depth, I give you my blessing to skip this chapter altogether.

- **The "20 Percent Extra" Edge:** By conducting some preliminary career research at this stage of the process, you can save yourself some time down the line and help yourself get focused a little faster.

- **"Go For It!" Bonus Activity:** To help you understand more about a particular career specialty, visit one of their professional association Web sites and read through recent conference agendas, educational opportunities, and press releases.

How to Prioritize Your Top Career-Change Choices

Ever gone shopping for something you wanted (clothes, a book, hiking equipment, whatever), and when you walked into the store there were so many possibilities you felt overwhelmed? When this happens to me, it usually takes me a few minutes to settle down and realize that, oh, there's a rack of items in the size I want. Or, over there are a few things in my price range. Pretty soon I discover that within the entire store of possibilities, there are just a few items that I really want to consider seriously.

Similar to my initial "settling down" experience in a store full of items, in this chapter, you're going to do some preliminary sorting and prioritizing of your Career Specialties to Consider to ultimately choose a few areas to investigate more in depth.

Gather Preliminary Information About Your Career Ideas

Learning more about your career ideas will help you decide which specialties you should take to the next step. The following resources can help you gather some preliminary career information:

- **Government career information sources:** America's Career InfoNet (www.acinet.org), the Occupational Outlook Handbook (www.bls.gov/oco), and the O*NET (www.onet.org) provide detailed descriptions for many career areas, including information about what working in a career would be like, training requirements, projected demand, and typical pay. While the information can be very helpful, realize that you probably won't find descriptions of some of the nichey specialties that interest you. For instance, these resources will provide you basic info about being a writer, but most likely you won't find specific information about working as a writer in the travel industry. For more information on industries, you can check the U.S. Department of Labor's Career Guide to Industries online at www.bls.gov/oco/cg/home.htm.

- **Books:** For more in-depth descriptions of specialized careers (such as, "Travel Writer"), check out Amazon.com (www.amazon.com) to locate books written about a particular career area.

- **Internet search engines:** If you're looking for still more info, run a career's keywords through an Internet search engine, such as www.google.com. For instance, type in "Planner for Car Shows," and then click through several of the citations to gather nuggets of information.

Panic Point! As you begin to learn more about specific career areas, you may uncover pieces of information that cause you concern. Maybe a career will require more training than you anticipated, or take longer to progress in than you'd expected. As these concerns pop up for you, be careful not to eliminate a career idea too quickly. Stop and ask yourself, "Does the majority of this career's description still seem appealing to me?" If your answer is "Yes!" then keep that career in the running, at least for now. In most cases, there are alternative—yet related—career options that you could choose to pursue within a particular career.

Refer to Your List of Values to Help in Your Decision-Making

Are you still fuzzy on which three career areas you should investigate further, even after conducting some preliminary research? Then it may be helpful to review your list from chapter 2 to see how well they align. For instance, Terrance, the Career Champ described in that chapter, created this values list:

1. Education

2. Helpfulness

3. Family

4. Security

5. Proactivity

6. Organization

7. Leadership

8. Abundance

9. Teamwork

10. Honesty

Using this list, Terrance could evaluate his career ideas by asking himself: "How well would Career Possibility #1 support my desire to keep learning? Be helpful to others? Allow me to balance work and family successfully? Give me a sense of security? Permit me to take proactive action on things? Operate in an organized manner? Lead others? Be compensated adequately? Be a part of a team? Conduct myself and my work honestly?" He could then ask himself the same questions related to his other career ideas, to see how well each idea supports his values.

Keep in mind that at this stage in the process, you won't know with complete certainty how well a career idea lines up with your values. You'll be guessing, to some degree, but that's okay. A career's match with your values will become clearer as you complete the activities in the next few chapters.

Choose Three Career Specialties to Investigate Further

Your goal at this stage in the process is to choose three career areas to investigate in more depth. If a particular career area seems in line with your top values, and if the initial information you gathered about that career area seems appealing, it's definitely worth considering as one of your top three.

Panic Point! Are you thinking, "None of these look like they'll work for me!" If this is where you're at, take a deep breath and keep reading. At this point in the process, it's normal to feel as though none of your initial ideas will work.

But what if *none* of your original ideas seems worth investigating further? What if you've had to eliminate every idea based on the preliminary information you've gathered? If this is the situation you find yourself in, don't panic. You're not the first person to run into this dilemma. Sometimes all it takes to move past this problem is to understand your career concerns a little more closely.

Complete the following statement about yourself: "When I consider choosing a few career areas to investigate further, I worry that...." Some Career Cowards worry that no career is ever going to give them what they want, so why even bother choosing a few ideas? Other people are concerned that if they decide on just a few ideas at this stage, they'll make the *wrong* choices or limit themselves from other choices later. And others fret that even though a career idea may seem intriguing, they may not be able to realistically make it happen.

Whatever your career concerns may be, I understand that they're very real to you. You don't want to make a wrong choice, so you may feel that it's safer to not make a choice at all! Yet please keep this in mind: At this stage in the career-change process, you're simply *considering and exploring.* You're not making any long-term decisions. As you gather more information, you'll begin to refine your career-choice options and gain more confidence in making the right choices for you. But *first* you need to get to the next step! So if you're struggling to pick three career ideas, look at your list right now and ask yourself, "Which three ideas—while not *perfect*—hold a spark of an interest to me right now?"

Then tell yourself, "I am in the process of exploring some career ideas. Even though it makes me a little nervous, I am simply considering a few possibilities at this stage. I may not see possibilities that meet *all* of my criteria yet, but I want to be able to move ahead to the next step—and ultimately to identify and change into a career area that is a better fit for me. So for now, I will choose three areas with which I can begin my research, simply as a place to start. Going forward, I reserve the right to change my mind about any career idea at any time. Bottom line, I am in control of my career choices."

You *will* have a chance to learn a great deal more about a number of career areas before you decide on any. You *will* get to evaluate which of them truly meet your needs. And you *will* feel much more confident about making career choices as we move further through this process. But for now, take a deep breath and choose three areas:

1. _____

2. _____

3. _____

Whew, you did it! Good for you. Now, moving on…

Why It's Worth Doing

There are literally hundreds of thousands of career specialties in our world today. You may wish you could thoroughly investigate each career possibility to find the *perfect* choice for you, yet it's simply not feasible. You'd spend your entire life wading through career information instead of deciding on and truly enjoying a few.

Yet the process you're working your way through—identifying and combining your talents, skills, interests, and values into a variety of career combinations, and then narrowing down your list to three career areas to begin investigating initially—has produced great results for thousands of people...even Career Cowards like you!

As uncomfortable as it may make you feel, choosing a few career areas to research—even if they don't look very likely for you at this point—will allow you to move further into the career-change process. This process of discovery might uncover even more ideas— ideas that haven't even entered your consciousness yet—which will be even *better* fits for you.

Career Champ Profile: Sheena

Sheena was frustrated with her Career Specialties to Consider list. "None of these look any good to me anymore," she told me. "Okay," I said, "when you think about investigating any of these careers further, what comes to mind for you, Sheena?" She took a deep breath and then sighed heavily. "I really don't want to work at all," she confessed. "When I retired from my job with the county, I thought I'd have enough money so that I didn't need to work, but it hasn't worked out that way. Now, as I've learned more about these ideas through my preliminary research, all I can think about is, 'These all look like too much work!'"

"What would you really rather be doing?" I asked her. "Traveling," she said, looking sad, "but I can't afford it right now." "Well, if you know that you *must* work, how about at least considering a few jobs that would somehow involve travel?" I suggested. On her list, Sheena had several Career Specialties to Consider that were related to travel. "Hmmmmmmm," Sheena began, "Well if I *have* to work, somehow being connected to travel might make it more bearable." She agreed to take Travel Information Specialist, Hotel Concierge, and Long-Term-Stay Property Manager to the next step in her career research.

Shortly thereafter, she discovered that the work involved in some of these specialties was actually pretty interesting to her, and her excitement started to grow. "If I can't travel right now, at least I can somehow be connected to travel through my work, and that seems acceptable to me for now," she decided.

Core Courage Concept

You're familiar with the saying, "The journey of a thousand miles begins with a single step," and this adage is especially true in career change. Moving into a new career is both exciting *and* terrifying. What challenges will you encounter as you move down the path? And will you be able to handle them?

While you won't truthfully know whether you can handle the challenges until you're faced with them, consider this: Would you rather stay where you are right now, safe...but miserable? Or are you willing to make some initial career decisions now and take the next step forward, so that ultimately you wind up in a much better place? One step at a time is all it takes to make progress.

Confidence Checklist

☐ Gather preliminary information about your career ideas.

☐ Refer to your list of values to help in your decision-making.

☐ Choose three career specialties to investigate further.

Chapter 6

Carry Out Some Career Experiments

Does the idea of being able to escape into a new career, just to try it out for a little while, seem appealing to you? Would you like to build your experience in a new specialty through fun, low-risk activities that might later help you move into that career more easily? If so, then you'll love the activities described in this chapter. You'll learn about, and have the opportunity to experience, several exciting career experiments that can bring you closer to your career-change goals.

Risk It or Run From It?

- **Risk Rating:** Zero to low, depending on what you choose to do.

- **Payoff Potential:** Very big. Career experiments allow Career Cowards to gather high-quality career information in a low-risk way. These activities can also help you bridge into a new career more easily and successfully.

- **Time to Complete:** An hour or more, again, depending on how much time and effort you choose to invest.

(continued)

(continued)

- **Bailout Strategy:** Career experiments aren't required, but they are a very good idea. If you decide to bypass career experiments, at least be sure to complete a number of the informational interviews as described in chapters 7 and 8.

- **The "20 Percent Extra" Edge:** Career experiments move you past the "looks good on paper" phase of changing careers (the step where most Career Cowards get stuck) and help you make true career-change progress.

- **"Go For It!" Bonus Activity:** Connect with instructors associated with training programs for your prospective careers, or contact members of professional associations and ask them for career experiment ideas. Because they're so immersed in their specialties, they should be able to come up with some awesome career-experiment ideas.

How to Choose and Execute Career Experiments

A career experiment can be one of thousands of activities that allow you to learn more about a new type of work *before* you commit to choosing it. Career experiments can range from simple, two-minute exercises that introduce you to important tidbits of information about that specialty, to more involved activities that may take several months to complete. Following is a list of sample career experiments, listed in order from least risky to activities that may require more confidence.

Begin with Internet Research to Get Your Career-Change Research Rolling

Finding career information on the Internet is a great way to begin your career experiments. Simply log on to your favorite search engine (my favorite is www.google.com), type in keywords connected to your career interest area, and see what you can uncover. For instance, I once typed in "asphalt earring design," just to see what kind of results a random set of keywords would produce. I actually found a number of Web sites describing earrings that were designed using asphalt. Just for fun (and to see what interesting career tidbits you can uncover), input keywords from your Career Specialties to Consider list. Here are a few tips for uncovering useful career info on the Internet:

- In addition to your keywords (such as "asphalt earring design"), try throwing in the keywords "career" and "association." Sometimes these keywords will help you uncover helpful training or career information Web sites.

- Alter your keywords slightly to see how your results change. For instance, rather than "design," you could try "designer"; or instead of "earring," you could try "jewelry."

- Maintain an open mind as you review the results. Sure, you'll uncover gazillions of irrelevant hits, but that's okay. Don't get discouraged too quickly. Keep poking around and trying new keyword combinations until you find a few useful references

Design Motivating Practice Projects That Build Your Confidence and Skills

As the name implies, practice projects are activities that allow you to experience a specialty without the pressure of having it be "for real." For example, let's say you've decided to investigate what it would be like to have a career as a tree-house builder. A logical practice project for this specialty would be for you to actually build a tree house. This doesn't mean that you need to run out to Home Depot and buy a truckload of lumber (although you could). If that seems like too big a step for you to take right away, there is a wide range of other practice projects that will allow you to learn more about this specialty.

For instance, you could begin by walking around your neighborhood to scope out trees that might be good candidates for a tree house. You could also pull out some paper and drawing tools and sketch a few ideas. If you like the idea of actually building a tree house, you could get your hands on a Bonsai tree and construct a miniature version of one of your designs. Or, if you want to jump in completely, go ahead and assemble a tree house in your own back yard.

When it comes to practice projects, it's usually best to start small and build momentum, so that you don't get too overwhelmed. Remember, although you may be excited to learn about a new career, it's still *new* to you. You're bound to experience a learning curve as you attempt to gain information about and execute the skills required for that specialty. Be kind to yourself and choose practice projects that allow you to begin with baby steps.

To design a practice project that will be a good fit for you, consider the following:

- Which career specialty do you want to research further?

- What key skills and activities are involved in this career?

- Which practice projects would allow you to experience some of these career activities? Ideas:

  - Make up a pretend case study and execute the related activities.

  - Use an Internet search engine to research real-life situations connected to that career specialty (such as inputting the keywords "tree house projects"), and then locate a small-scale activity you can execute yourself.

  - Using an Internet search engine, locate syllabus examples for training courses for a career specialty (input, "Syllabus X Class", with X being your career specialty), and review assignments suggested by the instructor.

  - If you're really drawing a blank, enlist the help of a creative friend or a career counselor for suggestions.

  - Brainstorm at least five possible practice projects and choose a few to execute.

Take Enlightening Field Trips to Boost Your Knowledge and Excitement

Remember the field trips we used to go on as grade-school students? My favorite was to a glass-making factory. I'll never forget the beautiful sculptures the glass blowers created. Thankfully, we're never too old for field trips! Expeditions like these allow you to learn more about the careers you're considering through fun, low-risk adventures.

Say for instance that you're researching a career as a planner of sales conferences and retreats. A fun field trip might involve traveling to hotels and conference centers that host those types of events. Once you're there, walk through the facilities on your own checking out rooms and resources, or request a tour from one of the representatives. If asked about your purpose, you can say, "I may be scheduling meetings here in the future," (which, if you ultimately choose that career path, is true) "and I want to know about the resources that are available."

Field-trip opportunities may exist through the following avenues:

- Visit businesses that hire people in the career you're researching. Again, if asked about your purpose you can say, "This type of work interests me. I just wanted to see where the action takes place."

- Visit organizations that provide supplies or services for the kind of work you're investigating.

- Visit a school that provides training for the career you're considering. Collect a course catalog and speak with an advisor about the programs offered. (Warning: After talking with an advisor, you may be tempted to sign up for training. Before you make that kind of commitment, be sure that you've researched the career thoroughly, to make sure it's a good fit for you.)

Shadow a Specialist to Further Confirm Your Interest

Want to learn more about a career, but don't want to have to perform in it quite yet? Then consider a job-shadow experience. Job shadowing allows you to observe a specialist in his or her work while you sit like a fly on the wall watching from the background.

Let's say that you're intrigued with the idea of a career as a computer programmer designing video games. One of the following job-shadow opportunities would give you the chance to see the action from the front lines:

- Through a local videogame programmers association, connect with a specialist and ask whether you can watch him at his work for two hours one day.

- Contact an area videogame programming school and request the opportunity to sit in a lab class as students work on a project.

- Check out your local job service center, library, or www.onet.org—a career information Web site—to see whether a video clip of a videogame programmer at work exists in the resource files.

If you choose job shadowing as one of your career experiments, observe the following guidelines to ensure a successful experience for both you and the specialist:

- Dress and act respectfully. If you're not sure of the dress code, phone the company's reception desk and ask.

- Ask permission before taking any notes or pictures.

- Remember, your role is as a "fly on the wall." Unless you're given the chance to speak or ask questions, keep quiet.

- Never, ever hint to the specialist about getting a job. Your purpose is research, not job search.

- Stick to the timeline you requested. If you asked to shadow a specialist for two hours, be prepared to leave at the end of that time.

- Always send a note thanking the specialist for the opportunity.

Volunteer to Gain Low-Risk, High-Reward Experience

Like the idea of gaining some real-world experience in a new career, but without the pressure of having to commit to it for the long term, or perform in it perfectly right away? Then volunteering may be an ideal career experiment for you. There are volunteer opportunities connected to nearly every career specialty.

If you like the idea of a career where you would be leading landscaping crews, you could obtain a volunteer opportunity that would allow you to gain that kind of experience through the following avenues:

- Contact your city or county landscaping department and describe the kind of volunteer experience you're hoping to gain. Chances are there are parks or other community grounds where you could be a part of a landscaping crew. Although you may not get to lead a group (at least right away), you'd still get some first-hand exposure to the work.

- Nonprofit establishments including churches, clubs, and social-service organizations, are frequently looking for specialized volunteer help. Call around to see what landscaping-leadership opportunities you can uncover.

- Launch your own landscaping project. Whether it's in your own yard, or a project for a needy friend or group, call together some supporters and implement a landscaping project of your own design.

- If you're having trouble coming up with a viable volunteer opportunity, contact your local library reference desk for ideas and referrals to groups in your area that may help you create the experience you seek.

Panic Point! Do you look at your list of Career Specialties to Consider and think, "I can't come up with a practice project, volunteer opportunity, or field trip for *any* of these! They aren't the type of careers that easily lend themselves to experiments!" You may be right; not every specialty provides career-experiment opportunities. (It would be difficult to actually try your hand at brain surgery, for example.) Yet most careers offer *some* kind of experiment possibilities (you *could* watch brain surgery on a medical show). If you're drawing a blank on any kind of experiment that would work for the career you want to research, step back and ask yourself, "Am I honestly unable to come up with an experiment, or am I putting up roadblocks for myself because of some other reason?" Fear about taking a step forward, for instance? Moving forward to gather career information can be *scary*, especially for Career Cowards. If you're feeling nervous, start small. Begin with Internet research. Once you've succeeded with that, consider moving on to a practice project you can execute on your own, and from there, progressing into experiments that feel more risky to you.

Why It's Worth Doing

You know how it goes…you think and think and think about changing careers, but day after day, week after week, year after year, you never really make any progress. You don't want to make a *wrong* move, but you're sick of being stuck and you're ready to make *something* happen.

Career experiments are the *perfect* step between having a career-change idea that excites you and jumping completely into a new career. Career experiments help you gather the information you need to make decisions that are right for you, so that ultimately, you succeed in making the career change you want.

Career Champ Profile: Kyle

For years Kyle thought about a career as an interior decorator. She even completed a bachelor's degree in fine arts while also working full-time in her job at a manufacturing company. She hoped her fine-arts degree would somehow land her in a creative career. But five years after she'd finished the degree, she was still working at the manufacturing company in a job that was anything but creative.

As frustrated as she was in her present work, she was nervous about taking a step forward into a new career. "What if I find out I'm not any good at interior decorating—that I can't make my dream come true? I'm nervous that if I try some of these career experiments, I'll be disappointed with what I find out about my opportunities."

Kyle's fear was a real one for her, but she didn't want to stay stuck in her frustrating job for the rest of her work life. Eventually she agreed to begin with some no-risk experiments. She input "interior decorating" into an Internet search engine and started poking around on some sites. "My design ideas are as good as some of the stuff I saw in the Internet," she reported to me the next week. "Okay, so how about going on a field trip next?" I suggested. After brainstorming some possibilities, she agreed to visit one of her favorite home-furnishings stores over the weekend, looking at the merchandise through the eyes of an interior decorator rather than just as a consumer.

At our next meeting, Kyle mentioned that Sheila, one of her friends, wanted to redo her living room. "But she's nervous about picking colors and fabric and furniture. I could help her, I guess," Kyle offered cautiously. "I think it's a great idea," I encouraged her. "Sheila is your friend. She's going to be supportive! Tell her up front that if she wants to brainstorm some ideas, you're willing, and that she's under no obligation to use any of your suggestions."

Kyle liked that idea, and as a practice project, she decided to inter-view Shelia about design styles she liked, looking through magazines with her. She then took things to the next step and designed an idea board similar to the design proposals she saw the professionals put together on television shows.

Two weeks later Kyle bounced into my office, full of excitement, with a large board tucked under her arm. "I brought my idea board with me," she announced. "It was *so fun* putting it together! Now I'm feeling much more confident about moving forward in my design career. This project with Sheila was fun, and I feel like I have some talent in this area. I'm researching online interior decorating courses right now. Once I get started in a training program, I'm going to line up an internship and make this career change happen!"

Core Courage Concept

Anyone can *talk* about changing careers, yet it takes courage to actually make it happen. By taking baby steps forward, through fun, doable career experiments, you allow yourself to begin building momentum through low-risk, high-payoff activities. Start small, pushing through your feelings of nervousness. Before you know it, your excitement will override your fear, and you'll be on your way to career-change success!

Confidence Checklist

☐ Begin with Internet research to get your career-change research rolling.

☐ Design motivating practice projects that build your confidence and skills.

☐ Take enlightening field trips to boost your knowledge and excitement.

☐ Shadow a specialist to further confirm your interest.

☐ Volunteer to gain low-risk, high-reward experience.

Part 3

Gather Essential Career Info and Make a Choice

Chapter 7

Master the Best-Kept Career-Change Secret: Informational Interviewing

O ver the years I've used a multitude of career tools—assessments, transition theories, how-to processes, you name it—and I've observed firsthand which resources deliver the best results. Informational interviewing, the technique you'll read about in this chapter, is by far the best tool I've found for helping people make effective progress toward changing careers. And because so few people seem to know about it and use it, I consider it my best-kept secret to successful career change. Once you've learned it and applied it, I believe you'll feel the same way, too.

Risk It or Run From It?

- **Risk Rating:** Slight. It feels more risky than it actually is.

- **Payoff Potential:** Beyond huge. This single activity can unlock the door to how to accomplish your successful career change.

- **Time to Complete:** A few hours or more, depending on how many interviews you choose to do.

(continued)

(continued)

- **Bailout Strategy:** I'd strongly recommend not skipping this step. It could easily mean the difference between succeeding or failing with your career change. But if for some very good reason you can't do it (such as if you're stranded alone on a desert island, with no phone, Internet, or mail service available to you) you could substitute a variety of the career experiments described in chapter 6.

- **The "20 Percent Extra" Edge:** By taking the time to interview individuals with expertise in a field that interests you, you move beyond the "Looks good on paper" phase of career change and begin to discover how to actually achieve your goals.

- **"Go For It!" Bonus Activity:** In addition to interviewing some local specialists, interview a few of the most accomplished professionals in the fields you're considering. Identify them by researching speakers at national conferences related to the careers that interest you. Often, the most proficient experts are some of the friendliest and most valuable resources you'll find.

How to Achieve Career-Change Success Through Informational Interviewing

Informational interviewing is the process of conversing with a specialist to gain an insider's view of what their career is truly like. Interviewing specialists in the career areas you're considering allows you to learn firsthand how they got started in their work, the pros and cons of their career, what kind of training they suggest, expected pay ranges, and typical career paths. This information can be highly useful in your career-change process because it helps you make better decisions and put together more successful career-transition plans.

For instance, several years ago I conducted an informational interview that changed my life. At that time I was working in my first career as a marketing specialist in the high-tech industry and was attending a professional-development workshop on how to be a better supervisor. While waiting for the class to begin, I looked through the workshop materials and read the biography of the presenter. She was described as a career counselor. I'd never heard of that title before, and the sound of it seemed especially appealing to me.

During one of the breaks I approached her excitedly and asked, "What do you do as a career counselor?" "I work one-on-one with adults helping them define and execute their career goals," she answered. "Do you like it?" I probed further. "Oh yes. It's very interesting. Every client is different, so there's lots of variety and I need to be creative in how I support them." "It sounds great!" I said. "Well," she offered, "It is pretty good, but there are downsides, too. Since I'm self employed, sometimes the pay is a little unpredictable. That's why I take on extra assignments, like leading these seminars. Plus occasionally I end up working with a client who is really stuck, and no matter what I try to do to help them, it doesn't work. That can be frustrating."

I thanked her for her information, and returned to my seat buzzing with excitement. I was especially jazzed by her description of the work as being creative and varied. And the idea of working for myself seemed exhilarating. I had experience with marketing and could see myself enjoying the process of promoting my business to help bring in enough income.

Even though I didn't realize it at the time, I'd just completed my first informational interview. After I'd become a career counselor myself, I realized how extremely valuable that single conversation had been to my career-change success, and now informational interviews have become a key step in the process I use with my own clients.

To make it work, though, you have to get past, "Me, talk to strangers? No way!"

Panic Point! At this point, most Career Cowards are thinking, "Interview strangers about their work? *Fat chance!* I'm *not* doing that." If the idea of talking with people you don't know about their work seems terrifying to you, *you're not alone.* A fear of informational interviewing is one of the most common fears in career change. But before you ditch this idea simply because it seems scary right now, please read through the next few chapters and at least *consider* the idea. Bottom line, no one can force you to conduct an informational interview (even though I'd like to be able to, because they're so valuable). At the very least, give yourself the chance to learn about informational interviews before you discard the idea altogether.

Here's the first important idea about informational interviewing I'd like you to consider: Almost always, specialists *like* to be asked about their work. Just imagine having someone approach you and say, "Your work seems very interesting to me. I'd like to ask you a few questions about it. Would that be okay?" Chances are your response would be, "Sure! Pull up a chair and let me tell you all about it!" People *love* talking about themselves, and an informational interview gives them an excellent opportunity to do just that.

And here's a second important idea: With informational interviewing, *you don't need to "sell" yourself.* Because the primary purpose of informational interviewing is *research,* not *job search,* you don't need to say anything impressive about yourself or try your best to get the specialist to hire you. Basically, you just need to ask questions and listen. Once you've conducted an informational interview or two, you'll see that it's really just a fun way to learn about careers that appeal to you.

Master an Effective Informational Interview Outline

Wonder what you'd ask a specialist about their work? Following is an informational interview outline that my clients have used thousands of times with excellent results.

Step 1: Introduce Yourself and Your Purpose

"My name is [NAME], and I'm considering changing careers. Currently I work in [CURRENT SPECIALTY], and I'm researching careers that may be a better match for me. Your work is interesting to me, and I'd like to learn more about it."

Step 2: Describe the Agenda and Gain Permission

"I have between 5 and 10 questions I'd like to ask you about your work. It should take between 15 and 30 minutes. Would it be okay if I take notes about what you tell me?"

Step 3: Ask Enlightening, Fun-to-Answer Questions

"How did you get into this career?"

"What do you like about it?"

"What are the downsides?"

"What does a typical day or week look like for you?"

"What skills or talents help you succeed in your work?"

"What sort of training is helpful?"

"How do people enter this line of work?"

"What are typical pay ranges for entry-level, mid-level, and senior-level experience?"

"Who else do you respect in this line of work that I should also interview?"

"If I have further questions about your work in the future, may I contact you again?"

Step 4: Listen, Take Notes, and Ask for Clarification

As you're conversing with the specialist, it's especially important to *keep the focus on the person you're interviewing.* As a guideline, the person you're interviewing should be talking 75 percent or more of the time.

Step 5: Follow Up

After the interview, send a thank-you note, and follow up with anyone to whom you've been referred. Figure 7.1 is a sample informational interview thank-you note.

Dear [THEIR NAME],

Thank you for taking the time to share information about your career. It was extremely interesting and will be very helpful in my career planning. Thank you also for your suggestion to interview [REFERRAL NAME]. I look forward to talking with him in the near future. If I can ever return the favor, please let me know.

Sincerely,

YOUR NAME

Figure 7.1: A sample thank-you note for an informational interview.

And here's a sample script to use when contacting the specialists to whom you've been referred:

> "Hello Mr./Ms. [NAME], My name is [YOUR NAME] and I was referred to you by [SPECIALIST NAME]. She spoke highly of your expertise in the field of [CAREER]. I am in the process of researching more about your work, as a potential career for myself in the future. Would you be willing to be interviewed about your work? The conversation would take between 15 and 30 minutes, and could be scheduled in person or over the phone at a time that is convenient to you."

Understand the Purpose Behind Some of the Questions

Sometimes Career Cowards question a few of the items I suggest in the informational interview outline. Specifically they wonder, "Do you really want to ask someone about the downsides of their job? Or about their pay? Or to be referred to other people? Aren't you asking an awful lot of them?" Although these questions can seem prying, if asked in a respectful way, most people are happy to answer them. Plus, the answers to the questions provide you critical information for making sound career-change decisions.

Ask someone about the downsides of their job, for instance, and typically the interviewee will be thrilled to enlighten you about the parts of their work they don't enjoy (wouldn't you be?). And wouldn't you rather know about the challenges in the work *before* you go to great lengths to switch into it? When it comes to pay, as long as you ask for *typical pay ranges*, rather than for specific details about what *they* make, people are usually happy to share the information. In regard to asking for referrals to other people within a career field, again, if you've conducted yourself in a respectful manner throughout the interview, the specialist will usually be happy to provide some referrals to other people they respect.

Although some of these questions may seem a little snoopy, view the process of informational interviewing as an experiment and try it to see what happens. I predict your outcome will be very good.

Find the Right People to Interview

Okay, now that you understand the purpose of an informational interview and what you would ask a specialist, you're probably wondering, "Yeah, but who do I interview? I don't know anybody in the career areas I'm researching." One or more of these techniques will help you identify some specialists:

- **Google an expert.** One of my favorite techniques for finding a specialist to interview within a career field is to input some keywords in your favorite search engine. For example, say you want to interview a city planner. You could input "City Planner" and "[SPECIFIC CITY NAME]." As with any search-engine query, you're bound to come up with several unrelated citations, but you should be able to find a number of useful ones as well.

- **Find a contact through a professional association.** Professional associations—groups of specialists within a career field who are organized to exchange information to advance their profession—exist for most career fields. Greenhouse managers, for instance, might be a member of the Nursery and Greenhouse Association. As someone interested in the field of greenhouse management, you could send an e-mail to the membership contact for an association, asking for a referral to a specialist you might interview. Active members of professional associations are typically very willing to assist someone interested in learning more about their profession. I've found professional associations to be perhaps the best avenue for locating specialists to interview. The association organizers can act as an effective liaison to connect you with leaders in the career field you're considering.

- **Ask for recommendations from people in your network.** Often a well-connected acquaintance, such as your insurance agent or accountant, can help you find specialists to interview. Because they interact with people in a variety of professions, they may know of people working in the career areas you want to investigate.

- **Tap into an instructor's or professor's knowledge.** Teachers offer another valuable avenue for locating specialists. Contact an instructor who teaches a course within the field you're investigating, and ask him or her for a referral to someone working in the field.

As you locate potential specialists, do your best to find someone who is actually working in the role that interests you, and not the boss or head of the department. Although talking to a department head may be helpful, you'll miss out on hearing some of the more detailed aspects of a specialty. Plus, you may one day need to contact that hiring manager as part of a job search, and it's better to hold off on meeting the decision maker until you're clear about your career plans.

Make Use of Easy Ways to Request Appointments

Your next big question is probably, "But how do I get past my fear of rejection to actually ask someone if I can interview them?" I know from experience that requesting an informational interview is a *very* scary step—one where many Career Cowards get stuck. Don't let this to happen to you! Consider the following techniques to find an interview-request strategy that fits your style:

- **Send an e-mail.** "Dear [SPECIALIST NAME], I learned of you through [RESOURCE]. I am researching more about [CAREER FIELD] as a potential career path for myself. To help with my decisions and planning, I am interviewing specialists such as yourself about your work. Would you be willing to be interviewed about your career? The conversation would take between 15 and 30 minutes and could be conducted in person or over the phone at time that is convenient to you. Please let me know, and if I haven't heard from you in a day or so, I will follow up with you to make sure you received this successfully."

- **Leave a voice mail.** Use the same script just mentioned, but phone the specialist and leave a voice mail at a time when they're unlikely to answer, such as before 7 a.m. or after 7 p.m.

- **Have a liaison make the initial request for you.** If you learned of a specialist through a well-connected acquaintance or professor, ask whether they would be willing to phone the specialist first to verify their willingness to be interviewed. After you get the go-ahead, then you can follow up to decide on the details. This is a method I've used with great success with my own clients. I will make the initial request of a specialist, and then have the client follow up. If you're working with a career counselor, you could also ask them for their help with this step.

Why It's Worth Doing

"Okay," you say, "so informational interviewing will give me more info about a career I'm considering. But is it really as important as she's making it out to be?"

In a word, YES! Over the years, I've talked with hundreds of people who want to change careers. Most of them say something like, "I have an idea for what I want in a career change, but I never seem to make any progress on it." I believe this is because they *never get past the looks-good-on-paper phase of the process*. They don't know what to do next to move forward, and they're too afraid to risk taking any wrong steps.

Informational interviewing solves both of these problems beautifully. By interviewing specialists with expertise in a career field that interests you, you gather detailed information that is much more realistic than guessing what a career *might* be like. These details help you make better decisions, *plus* they give you a clear picture of what it will truly take for you to succeed in a new career. Can you actually execute the change you're imagining…and do you honestly want to? Informational interviewing allows you to answer both of these important questions with confidence.

Career Champ Profile: Paul

Paul was frustrated. He was in his mid-twenties, ready to get his career on a good path, but didn't know which path that should be. After high school, he'd completed an associate's degree in electronics and worked as a engineering technician at a computer manufacturing company for a few years. Although Paul enjoyed the work and was good at it, he quickly learned that without further education, his career options were limited. He also learned that the high-tech industry was volatile and unpredictable. Within the three years he worked as an employee, the company conducted two layoffs. Paul felt as if he was holding his breath every day he went to work, wondering whether he'd receive his layoff notice that day.

In an effort to create a more secure future for himself, Paul completed a course to become a certified real-estate appraiser. Yet he discovered shortly after landing his first position in his new field that that nature of the work didn't suit his personality well. Paul had imagined that the work would be exacting and measurable, allowing him to precisely evaluate a property's worth. Yet he discovered that in the world of real estate, appraisals could be highly subjective and political. Frustrated, he quit that career, too, and took an in-between job as an upholsterer working at an auto-repair shop until he could figure out his next step.

"I want to find something that's a good, long-term fit for me," Paul told me. He agreed to conduct a series of informational interviews that would allow him to understand a career field in-depth before he committed to it, because he didn't want to make the same mistake he'd made with his appraisal career choice.

As he began his informational interviews, his top three career interests were audio engineer, installing and repairing in-home sound systems; electronics engineer, working on computers; and manufacturing engineer, planning and implementing efficient manufacturing processes.

Paul had his first informational interview with an electronics engineer, and after that conversation quickly decided to eliminate that career possibility. "I thought that working as an engineer, rather than as a technician, might give me more career stability. But those guys have to put up with the same threat of layoffs that I did. Plus they spend a lot of time staring at a computer screen, and that doesn't appeal to me. I like something that is much more hands-on."

Paul's interview with a manufacturing engineer was a little more interesting. "I like that they get to work with equipment and move around a lot on the job. But I'm still uncomfortable with putting my career future in the hands of an employer who could lay me off whenever they choose."

Through his informational interviews, it was becoming clearer to Paul that he might want to work for himself, allowing himself to keep the fate of his future in his own hands. His third informational interview, with a self-employed audio engineer, confirmed this hunch. "I liked that the audio engineer was in control of his own employment destiny. Yet I'm not convinced that I want to be an audio engineer. According to the guy I interviewed, he has to scramble to find jobs, and I want to make enough money to support a family."

Paul had eliminated his first three career possibilities, so he went back to his career compass for other ideas. He was also interested in home security systems, so Paul interviewed an owner of a home-security business and came away from the conversation highly excited.

"That guy really loves his work, and he says the field is growing so fast that it's fairly easy to land jobs. I would need to work as an apprentice for a few years, but I like that idea. Not only can I master how to become a home-security specialist, but I can also observe what it takes to run a successful business at the same time." Paul was well on his way to defining a satisfying career-change path for himself.

Core Courage Concept

Although it can seem safer to hold a career idea close to you and not risk losing it by looking at it too closely, ultimately you won't make any progress toward achieving your career goals. Even though the thought of interviewing specialists about their work might seem terrifying, doing so can help you take that precious career idea and grow it into something that actually allows you to achieve the career goals you want.

Confidence Checklist

- ☐ Get past, "Me, talk to strangers? No way!"
- ☐ Master an effective informational interview outline.
- ☐ Understand the purpose behind some of the questions.
- ☐ Find helpful people to interview.
- ☐ Make use of easy ways to request appointments.

Chapter 8

Execute a Successful Informational Interview

So you made it through chapter 7 and haven't run away screaming at the idea of an informational interview. Good for you! Hang in here, because in this chapter you'll learn step-by-step details about how to execute a successful informational interview, from what to wear, to what to say, to how to follow up after the meeting. Follow the details suggested in this chapter and your informational interviews will be smooth and successful.

Risk It or Run From It?

- **Risk Rating:** Still relatively minimal. Follow the recommendations in this chapter for low-risk, high-payoff results.

- **Payoff Potential:** Again, massive. Effective informational interviews can mean the difference between success and failure when it comes to successful career change.

- **Time to Complete:** A few hours or more.

- **Bailout Strategy:** If you've gotten this far, why not keep going? But if you must bail, execute several of the career experiment activities in chapter 6.

(continued)

(continued)

> - **The "20 Percent Extra" Edge:** A well-executed informational interview is enjoyable for both you and the specialist, allowing you to have a successful, informative experience.
>
> - **"Go For It!" Bonus Activity:** Want to be extra-sure that your informational interviews will go as well as possible? Conduct a practice interview with someone who supports your career-change goals, and consider recording yourself to review for improvements.

How to Implement a Successful Informational Interview

You already learned the basics of informational interviewing in chapter 7. Now you'll gain knowledge about many of the more subtle, yet very important, aspects of executing a successful informational interview—such as what to do if you don't hear back about your request, how much to talk, how to handle a surprise job offer, and more.

Set Up Your Informational Interview Appointments

When you phone or e-mail a potential resource, a script like this communicates your request clearly and quickly:

> "Dear [SPECIALIST NAME], my name is [YOUR NAME], and I learned of you through [RESOURCE]. I am researching more about [CAREER FIELD] as a potential career path for myself. To help with my decisions and planning, I am interviewing specialists such as yourself. Would you be willing to be interviewed? The conversation would take between 15 and 30 minutes, and could be conducted in person or over the phone at a time that is convenient to you. I would want to ask you questions such as how you got into your work, pros and cons, training that is helpful—that kind of thing. Please let me know if you would be willing to be interviewed. I can be reached at

[YOUR NUMBER]. If I haven't heard from you in a day or so, I will follow up with you to make sure you received this message successfully."

What if the specialist doesn't reply to your first request within a day or two? If this happens, don't panic. Actually, you're in the majority! In my experience, most specialists asked to be interviewed don't reply to the first request. This is sad but true. I believe it's because, just like you, they're a little nervous about talking with a stranger. Almost always when I'm making an informational interview request for a client, or if a client is making one for himself, it requires at least two (and sometimes three) attempts to hear back from the specialist.

If you haven't heard back on your first request within two business days, follow up, only this time use a different communication method if possible. For instance, if you sent an e-mail first, make a phone call this time (remember, you can call before or after regular business hours to minimize the chance of having the specialist answer). You can use a script such as this one:

"Hello, [Mr./Ms. LAST NAME]. This is [YOUR NAME], and I'm following up on an e-mail I sent a few days ago. It was a request to see whether you would be willing to be interviewed about your work. I wasn't sure if my message got through successfully, so I wanted to check back. I'm researching a potential career change for myself, and your career is interesting to me. I'm wondering whether I could interview you, in person or over the phone, for 15 to 30 minutes at a time that is convenient to you. I have between 5 and 10 questions I'd like to ask, such as how you got into your work, good parts and bad parts, and training that would be helpful. Please let me know if this would be okay with you. My phone number is [YOUR NUMBER]; again, that's [YOUR NUMBER], or you can e-mail me at [YOUR EMAIL]. Thank you in advance for your consideration of my request."

And what if they still don't reply to you within a day or two? Well, you need to follow up one more time—you pick the method, e-mail or voice mail—to wrap things up and give them a graceful out. It's important to do this because you may cross paths with them at some point in the future (especially if you decide to move into their line of work) and you don't want your unanswered request to be an awkward issue between the two of you. Follow up with a message like this one to allow the specialist to save face if the two of you ever do meet:

> "Hello, [Mr./Ms. LAST NAME]. I just wanted to follow up one last time about my request to interview you about your work. This may be an especially busy time for you, so I'll make this my last request. If you ever do have time to talk in the future, or if you can suggest someone else that I might interview, please call me at [YOUR NUMBER]. Thank you for your time and consideration, and I wish you continued success in your career."

Panic Point! Do you worry you'll be a pest by contacting them more than once? Although it's true that you don't want to hound them, leaving unfinished business between you and a potential colleague creates an uncomfortable situation. Imagine running into them in the future. How awkward! For this reason, it's essential that Career Cowards maintain professionalism and allow their contacts a graceful out. Keep in mind that many things may get in the way of a specialist responding to you. They could be on an extended leave, your messages may not be getting through, or they could be especially busy at work. Whatever the reason, by following up with them you allow them to save face and preserve your future relationship.

And remember, if your first attempt to line up a specialist for an informational interview doesn't pan out, make the same request with another specialist. *The vast majority of people are happy to be interviewed about their work.* If the first person you asked wasn't receptive, chances are very good that the next person will say yes. And the persistence you demonstrate with this step in the process—by not giving up, and by asking someone else—will help you succeed with other career-change challenges you encounter in the future.

Know What to Wear, Where to Meet, How to Act

The specialist you asked for an informational interview has said, "Yes!" So now what? Set yourself up to succeed with the following arrangements:

- **Determine whether you'll be meeting in person or over the phone.** ["Mr./Ms. LAST NAME], would you prefer to meet in person or over the phone? I could come to your office, we could meet at a nearby coffee shop, or we could schedule a phone appointment. What would work best for you?"

- **Decide on a time that works for both of you.** If possible, most people prefer to meet during regular business hours, between 8 a.m. and 5 p.m. However, that may not be possible because of your work schedule. In this case, do what you can to accommodate the specialist: ["Mr./Ms. LAST NAME], I am finished with work at 5:30 p.m., and I could talk with you sometime after that, if that would work for you. I am also available during the weekend. Which time do you prefer?"

- **Double-check the appointment time and place.** Once you've decided on a meeting, repeat the details: "So, I'm planning to meet you at Mugs Coffee Shop on Smith Street at 5:30 p.m. this coming Thursday, April 19." If you're planning to talk on the phone, decide who will be calling whom. If it's a long-distance call, you should bear any charges yourself. And be sure to take into account any difference in time zones.

- **Dress appropriately.** If you're meeting in person, aim to look neat, but don't dress as if you're going in for a job interview. In most cases, a nice pair of slacks and a collared shirt will be sufficient. Add a blazer or jacket if you want, but skip the interview suit!

- **Take notes (and leave your resume at home).** Since you're conducting research, you'll want to have a notepad and something to write with. Some people like to use a recorder. If you're a terrible note taker, this may be a good idea. Whichever method you choose, be sure to ask the specialist for permission to take notes or to record the conversation. But leave your resume at home. Remember, the purpose of this meeting is for *research*, not *job search*. You don't want to present a mixed message. If the specialist asks for your resume, say something like, "Because I'm still deciding on my future career path, I haven't created my resume yet. However, I'll be happy to keep you posted on my decisions and share one with you at a later time. Would that be okay?"

- **Turn off distractions.** Your cell phone, Blackberry, or any other beeping device should be turned off so that you can give the specialist your full attention.

- **Be an effective listener.** As the interviewer, you should talk 25 percent or less of the time, and listen for 75 percent or more of the conversation. Make frequent eye contact, nod your head to show you understand, and ask appropriate follow-up questions such as, "Please tell me more about that part," or "Would you elaborate on the X aspect of your work?" If there's something you want to say while the specialist is talking, rather than interrupt, make a note of it and bring it up during a break in the conversation.

- **Use an agenda.** It's perfectly fine to take along a list of questions. In fact, the interviewer will be impressed that you're prepared! It's also fine to share a copy of the questions with the specialist at the beginning of the conversation. This sometimes helps the specialist to stay focused with his or her responses.

- **Keep track of the time.** You've asked for 15 to 30 minutes, so be sure to watch the clock. Keep your timepiece in clear view so that you know how much time you have left. As you near the end of your prearranged timeframe, say, "I asked for 30 minutes, and I want to be respectful of your time. Should we wrap up now, or should we keep talking?" It's very likely that the specialist will want to keep on talking, because he or she will be having so much fun sharing the details of his or her work. If they want to keep talking (and people often do...I've known informational interviews to continue for 90 minutes or more), and if you have the time, go for it!

- **Handle "want a job?" offers.** Sometimes a specialist is so impressed with the fact that you have interest in their career that they may offer you a job. Being offered a job during an informational interview can be flattering and exciting, but be wary of saying, "Yes!", at least right away. Keep in mind that you're still researching and making decisions about your career path. It's better to respond with, "Wow, I'm really flattered. Thank you! Because I'm still researching my career path, I'm not ready to make that kind of decision right now. Could I get back to you in the near future, once I'm clearer about my plans?" The specialist will be impressed with your commitment to making a decision that's right for you, and if they really want to hire you, they'll be willing to wait.

- **Wrap up successfully.** Review your questions and notes to make sure you've covered everything. Confirm the contact information for any referrals you've been given, ask for their business card, and look the specialist in the eye and say, "This has been very helpful to me, thank you. May I keep in touch if I have further questions, and to let you know how things progress for me?"

- **Send a timely thank-you.** Whether it's an e-mail or a hand-written note (either is fine), it's important to send a message thanking the specialist for his or her time and insights (see figure 8.1).

Mr. [SPECIALIST],

Thank you so much for allowing me to interview you about your work. It was especially helpful to me at this stage in my career research. I particularly enjoyed hearing about the X aspect of what you do. Thank you also for the suggestion to contact [Ms. REFERRAL]. I will follow up with her in the near future. As we discussed, I will keep you posted on my career progress. Again, thank you, and if I can ever return the favor, please let me know.

Sincerely,

[YOUR NAME]

Figure 8.1: An informational interview thank-you note.

Why It's Worth Doing

A well-executed informational interview makes the experience comfortable and pleasant for both you and the specialist. Sure, it takes some courage to follow up if you haven't heard back about your first request—but you'll come across as an impressive professional if you do. And although it may seem like a lot of steps to prepare an agenda, request permission to take notes, and practice your best listening skills, the extra care you put into creating a successful meeting will pay off with helpful information *plus* the opportunity to make a positive impression with a potential future colleague.

Career Champ Profile: Joel

"Richard didn't respond to my e-mail about my request for an informational interview," Joel reported anxiously in our career-counseling session. Joel had been referred to Richard by a professor at the local college as someone with expertise as a sales support specialist in the printing industry. "It probably means he doesn't want to be bothered."

Joel had been working in a telemarketing center for the past two years. A few months before, he'd finished a degree in business administration and was eager to put his new training to use in a job that was more in line with his interests. I'd encouraged Joel to conduct some informational interviews to help him decide where within the business world he wanted to focus his career. Joel understood the value of informational interviewing, but he was still nervous about actually meeting with specialists.

"Did you phone him with a second request?" I asked. "I don't want to hound the guy," Joel responded. I reminded him that there were several possible reasons why Richard hadn't yet responded to his e-mail. "Maybe it never even got through. Or he's been out of the office. Or he didn't completely understand what you were asking of him. Whatever the reason, you don't want to leave this loose end hanging. How about if you call Richard tonight after 7 p.m., when he's unlikely to answer, and leave him a voice mail with a second request?"

Joel reluctantly agreed. When we talked the next week, Joel's anxiety had turned to excitement. "So I called him like you suggested, and guess what? He'd accidentally deleted my e-mail and was glad that I followed up. We actually met on Monday this week."

Joel told me how they'd gotten together at a Starbucks after work, and how willing Richard had been to answer his questions. "I did a good job of listening, like not interrupting when I had something I wanted to say. I just made a note of my comment and brought it up later. And wow, Richard's work sounds *really* interesting. I like how his projects change from week to week, and how he gets to troubleshoot problems with customers." Richard had even referred Joel to another sales support specialist at a different printing company. "I'm going to set up that informational interview next. This is exciting. I feel like I'm making great progress toward creating what I want in a career!"

Core Courage Concept

Informational interviews can seem overwhelming. Contacting and talking with strangers seems so *scary*. Yet you *can* do it, especially considering that you've got great scripts and techniques to help make your informational interviews a success. Setting up and conducting informational interviews may be one of the most courageous moves you ever make for yourself—and imagine where it can take you! That single step can trigger a series of events that lead to a lifetime of increased career successes and satisfaction.

Confidence Checklist

- [ ] Set up your informational interview appointments.
- [ ] Determine whether you'll be meeting in person or over the phone.
- [ ] Decide on a time that works for both of you.
- [ ] Double-check the appointment time and place.
- [ ] Dress appropriately.
- [ ] Take notes (and leave your resume at home).
- [ ] Turn off distractions such as cell phones and Blackberries.
- [ ] Be an effective listener.
- [ ] Use an agenda.
- [ ] Keep track of the time.
- [ ] Handle "want a job?" opportunities.
- [ ] Wrap up successfully.
- [ ] Send a timely thank-you.

Chapter 9

Get Unstuck (If You Are)

Y ou've taken some big steps in this process so far (or at least thought about them). You've identified talents and skills you want to use, as well as passion zones that can help you home in on work that is both meaningful and interesting to you. You've defined what's important to you in your life to help you make solid, successful career decisions. You've put this information together to create a starter list of career ideas to consider. And (hopefully) you're now taking those ideas to the next step, by investigating them through career experiments and informational interviews.

But are you feeling a little stuck with this part? If so, you're not alone. Many Career Cowards hesitate when it comes to moving forward in their career research. The following techniques can help you break through your fear and make true progress with your career change.

Risk It or Run From It?

- **Risk Rating:** Zilch to very low. But some of these ideas may make you squirm a little.

(continued)

(continued)

- **Payoff Potential:** Whopping, especially if these steps help you break through your blocks and move forward.

- **Time to Complete:** Most of these ideas take just a minute or two to implement.

- **Bailout Strategy:** If you're not stuck, turn to chapter 10. If you are stuck, another approach would be to talk with someone you trust—a mentor, counselor, or good friend—to help you troubleshoot your stuck-points.

- **The "20 Percent Extra" Edge:** Most career-change wannabes never actually work through their challenges. They hit a wall and say, "Well, I tried, but it didn't work. Guess I'll stay where I am, even though I'm miserable." However, if you run into a roadblock and say, "Hey, look what I encountered. How will I handle it?" and then troubleshoot it, you begin to program yourself for one success after another.

- **"Go For It!" Bonus Activity:** Keep a log of the career-change challenges you encounter, as well as how you handled them. In the future, as you run into new roadblocks, you can easily remind yourself of the many times you were able to triumph over your challenges.

How to Move Past Your Own Personal Roadblocks

One or more of the following techniques can help you get unstuck and keep your career-change process moving forward successfully.

Determine the Worst Possible Outcome and Weigh the Risks

Let's say that you're considering e-mailing a specialist to request an informational interview—but your fear of looking silly is keeping you from doing it. Ask yourself, "What's the worst possible thing that could happen by taking this step?" Well, the specialist could read your e-mail, throw back his head, laugh hysterically, and then e-mail you with a "no way!" reply. Or that specialist could spread the word among his colleagues that he thinks you're a dope for making such a request (although in reality, he would be the one who looked like a dope, by criticizing someone for wanting to gather some helpful career information). Another outcome might be that he doesn't answer you at all. Would you be able to survive these possible results?

Now think about the next career step you want to take, and imagine the worst possible outcome. Can you live through it? Is it worth risking? If so, go for it.

Break the Step into More Manageable Pieces

So you're thinking about conducting a career experiment, such as creating a sample Web site to see what it would be like to have a career as a Web developer. But you feel overwhelmed by this idea because right now, you know *nothing* about Web-site creation (you feel lucky that you even know how to turn on your computer!). To make the task more manageable, you could break this career experiment into smaller steps such as these:

1. Pick a topic for the Web site.

2. Use an Internet search engine to research sites that have been created for organizations with similar topics.

3. Print a few Web pages that you like and whose ideas you might want to incorporate into your project.

4. Take a field trip to a store that sells Web-development software and show a sales rep the Web-page samples you printed as examples of the kind of programming you'd like to be able to do. Ask him or her for recommendations on software.

5. Research books, classes, or tutorials that could help you learn the software the rep recommended.

6. Decide on an option that will help you learn something about Web programming.

7. Attempt to create a small piece of your sample Web site using free trial software.

8. If you get stuck, find help, such as the helpline for the software you're using, an instructor, or someone who has used the Web-programming software.

9. Create another small piece of your sample Web site and continue to build your skills.

10. Complete the Web site!

As you consider the steps involved in your own overwhelming task, keep asking yourself, "How can I break this step into even smaller pieces?" Keep dissecting the step until you determine a starting point that you're willing to tackle.

Reward Yourself

Years ago, during my career as a marketing specialist, one of my responsibilities was to call customers to find out what they thought about our products. We then used this information for advertising and new product development. But I learned quickly that when I called customers, there was the chance that they were unhappy with our products, and I would be the person who got to hear about all of their frustrations.

After a while, I began to dread making those customer calls…but I knew I had to do it. That's when I discovered the motivational power of Peanut M&Ms. I would open a bag, line up several candies on my desk where I could easily see them, and tell myself, "You can have one Peanut M&M for every customer call you make." It was a simple (and pretty silly) motivation system, but it worked!

On the flip side, some Career Cowards are more motivated by what they might *lose* than by what they could *gain*. For example, one of my clients told herself that if she failed to complete a key step toward her career change by Friday of each week, she would have to donate one of her favorite items of clothing to charity. Rather than forfeit all of her best outfits, she began to take more risks in her career change, and ultimately achieved great career-change results.

As you think about a career-change step that intimidates you, what reward or risk will motivate you? Would it be treating yourself to a latte after you send an e-mail? Or not allowing yourself to lose your privilege of a weekly movie rental? Determine what spurs you to action and then use it to your advantage.

Define Your Challenge and Then Talk to an Expert

If your challenge seems more personal than career related, it might be helpful to talk with a counselor or therapist. For example, there was a time when I took a fairly big risk at work (I tried to launch an infomercial) and it failed. After that, I felt as if everything I touched would be unsuccessful. That fear-of-failure feeling caused me to stop doing even simple things that would keep my business running smoothly. I talked with a counselor about my problem and she described my situation as being caught in a Shame Spiral, where the embarrassment I felt over an error was leaking into other areas of my life. Talking with the therapist helped me put the failure into perspective and regain my willingness to take reasonable risks again. Counseling services may be available to you for little or no cost through local social-service organizations, or ask people you trust for recommendations to a therapist.

Panic Point! Feel so overwhelmed that you're paralyzed to take any steps at all, even baby ones? Then it may make sense for some Career Cowards to talk to an expert to get some one-on-one support and input. Specialists who help others deal with fear and change can often help you identify the specific issue that's holding you back and help you move past it. You may want to begin by checking with your local job service or workforce center. They have career counselors on staff with expertise in helping individuals achieve their career objectives, and often there is no charge to use their services. Your college or trade school career center may also be a resource for you.

Give Yourself a Deadline

Some of us work best under pressure. Jim, a career changer who wanted to conduct some informational interviews but was nervous about contacting specialists, used a stopwatch to help him follow through. He'd turn on the timepiece and then give himself no more than two minutes to make the call. It worked!

Analyze Your Other Successful "Firsts"

Often, the first time you attempt a task it can seem especially scary, yet after you've been through it once, you discover it wasn't such a big deal after all. To help you move ahead on a "first" that seems daunting to you, see if you can identify five other firsts in your life that you've successfully overcome. Instances that come to mind for me are riding a bike (that memory is still very clear), traveling outside of the United States (to France at age 15), balancing my checkbook (after bouncing several checks during my freshman year at college), rollerblading with my dog (we've had a few mishaps, but it's been fun), and writing and submitting a book proposal (that one seemed *really* scary). Now, however, these activities seem doable and almost routine to me.

Create your own list of firsts to remind yourself that even though a task once seemed overwhelming and frightening at the time, you *did* succeed, and you can succeed again!

Try It Just Once

Along the same line of "firsts," challenge yourself to try an intimidating task just once. If you decide it was just too terrible to repeat, at least you'll have the satisfaction of knowing you gave it a try.

Remember, for Now You're Just Exploring!

This is a *very* important point. Career Cowards often get themselves into a tizzy by thinking they have to take the exact right step with every career move they make. Yet the career-change process is by nature highly inexact. It can be compared to a scientist trying to discover a solution to a problem. She will experiment with several possible combinations of elements, making adjustments along the way, until she hits upon a successful formula. The idea that she would instinctively know the correct remedy at the start of her process is ridiculous!

Similarly, you are trying to find the formula to solve your own career-change challenge. There are many factors involved, so your process is bound to take some trial and error. Allow yourself to experiment and make mistakes. Each failure will provide you new information for improving your chances of success next time.

Build Momentum with Small Steps First

Not yet willing to take a step that seems daunting to you? It's okay to set it on the back burner for now. Instead, determine several smaller steps you can take to help yourself build momentum. For instance, if the idea of asking a specialist for an informational interview seems scary to you, take care of some of the smaller details first. Write a script of what you will say when you make the request. Practice the script to yourself several times. Scope out a coffee shop where you might meet for the interview. Pick out the outfit you might wear. Write up your questions. Buy your thank-you-note stationery. As you succeed with these baby steps, you build your confidence for eventually taking the bigger leap.

Practice with a Friend

If the thought of meeting with a stranger to interview him or her about their work sends you into a panic, it might help to first practice the interview with someone who seems more familiar. Ask a friend or family member whether you can interview them about their work. Once you've completed your dress rehearsal, chances are you'll discover that the meeting is fun and enlightening for both of you, and you'll be motivated to try it out with a specialist in a career area that truly interests you.

Why It's Worth Doing

Being stuck can feel like having a ball and chain around your ankle; you struggle to make progress, but the weight of your burden holds you back and drains your energy. Troubleshooting and moving past your stuck-points is like cutting off that ball and chain. Suddenly, you feel so much freer and lighter, as if you could accomplish anything!

Even if it's just a small challenge that you conquer, breaking through stuck-points boosts your confidence (even if it's just a little). And instead of letting your fears hold you back *forever,* you learn to achieve and live the life you really want—one tiny success at a time.

Career Champ Profile: JoEllen

JoEllen felt stuck. She'd identified five career areas that looked appealing to her and conducted some initial research, including looking up information on the Internet and reading a book about careers in the medical industry. But after that she'd hit a wall. She didn't feel comfortable making a decision about which career path to choose, but the idea of informational interviews terrified her. "I'm so afraid I'll sound like an idiot!" she confessed to me, close to tears.

"Okay, let's analyze this a little further. What's the worst thing that could happen if you requested an informational interview with a specialist?" I asked her.

JoEllen described her fear of stumbling over her words when she made the phone call. "I've been known to say stupid things when I'm nervous," she explained. I suggested that she write a word-for-word script of what she might say, practice it to herself several times, and then call and practice it on me. "Then you can decide whether you want to risk calling a real informational interview contact." She committed to following through on those action items.

The next time we talked she was feeling better about her ability to come across well over the phone, but she still hadn't made any calls.

"How about coming up with a reward for yourself if you make a call?" I suggested. Right away JoEllen perked up. "Oh, there's this cute purse I saw last weekend that I'd love to buy, but I really don't *need* it. Still, if it was a reward for doing something scary like this, maybe I could justify getting it for myself."

On my voice mail the next morning was a message from JoEllen. "I got my purse!" she began excitedly. "Plus I set up an informational interview. I'm so proud of myself!"

Core Courage Concept

Most times when we try something new, it feels uncomfortable. This is perfectly normal, although we may not like it. Learning something new requires us to push outside of our comfort zone into unknown territory. Often, we aim to protect ourselves from potential harm by backing away from new experiences. But retreating over and over again can cause us to feel stuck and frustrated.

As ideas in this book make you squirm with fear, be kind to yourself and understand why you feel ill-at-ease. Then tell yourself, "I've succeeded with many things in my life before, and I can succeed with these challenges also. Some of them may make me uncomfortable, but I'm going to push through my fear and go for it anyway."

Confidence Checklist

☐ Determine the worst possible outcome and weigh the risks.

☐ Break the step into more manageable pieces.

☐ Reward yourself.

☐ Define your challenge and then talk to an expert.

☐ Give yourself a deadline.

☐ Analyze your other successful "firsts."

☐ Try it just once.

☐ Remember, for now you're just exploring!

☐ Build momentum with small steps first.

☐ Practice with a friend.

Chapter 10

Gather Info and Make Choices

A s you execute career experiments and informational interviews, you'll gather valuable bits of information—both encouraging *and* discouraging—about the career areas you're considering. This section provides you tips for how to process that information to keep making steady progress toward your career-change goals.

Risk It or Run From It?

- **Risk Rating:** Low to mid-range; you'll begin to prioritize your opportunities now.

- **Payoff Potential:** Excellent! Good decisions now lead to great career results later.

- **Time to Complete:** The "gathering information" part could take hours or months, the synthesizing data and decision-making piece of it...well, the right choice could come to you in an instant!

- **Bailout Strategy:** If you're rock-solid sure of your career-change choice, skip this chapter.

- **The "20 Percent Extra" Edge:** When it comes to important decisions, most people avoid making them altogether, or

---

(continued)

(continued)

> take a wild guess and hope for the best. This process of gathering and evaluating data will allow you to make first-rate decisions for yourself through a proven, step-by-step process.
>
> - **"Go For It!" Bonus Activity:** Begin to keep a diary or record of your insights as you collect and process career information. Very quickly you'll see how much progress you're making toward your career-change goals, as well as help yourself become more clear about the decisions you want to make.

How to Collect and Process Helpful Career-Change Info

So you've completed some career experiments and have begun interviewing specialists for information. Congrats! Insightful career-change clues are now coming your way. Learn how to process this data to support your successful career-change result.

Make a Pros and Cons List

A simple and effective method for collecting and processing your field research data is a pros and cons list. Say for instance that you've just interviewed a real-estate assistant about his work. He described how much he liked the variety and fast pace. Plus he liked being able to use his computer skills to keep track of client information and to create Web pages and flyers about properties.

He also talked about how it was sometimes difficult to find full-time work because most real-estate agents don't need an assistant 40 hours per week. Another downside he mentioned was how sometimes his real-estate-agent boss would get very stressed right before a property closing.

After this conversation, you spend a few minutes analyzing the pluses and minuses of what you've just learned, *as they pertain to your career priorities* (which may be different from the priorities of the specialist you interviewed). For instance, whereas the assistant you interviewed doesn't like the part-time nature of the work, this aspect of the profession may fit your desired lifestyle perfectly. And whereas the assistant said he likes the fast pace of the work, that may not be your cup of tea. So in this situation, a pro/con list for *you* about this profession may look something like this:

Pros of Being a Real-Estate Assistant	Cons of Being a Real-Estate Assistant
• I could work part time.	• Fast pace (I like things more slow and steady)
• There's a lot of variety in the work.	• Having the agent get stressed sometimes (again, I like things calm and low-key)
• I could create Web pages and flyers on the computer (I love that kind of thing!).	

As you gather more information about a particular career from different specialists, keep a running list of the advantages and disadvantages of each career area you investigate.

Refer to Your Prioritized List of Values Often

The volume of career information you gather can seem overwhelming. How do you sort through all of the details to decide whether a career is truly a good fit for you? Your prioritized list of values (from chapter 2) can help you stay on track for making solid decisions. Let's say, for instance, that you've just discovered that one of the career areas you're considering would require you to learn a second language. At first you may think, "Oh no! It would be so much work to learn a second language!" But then you look at your prioritized list of values and see that #2 on your list is Learning. "Hmmm," you think, "since I love learning, why not learn a language?" Your prioritized list of values can help you analyze new career data in an objective, methodical way.

Be Honest with Yourself

Sometimes Career Cowards want to sugar-coat the information they gather to make it fit the dream career they've been imagining. For instance, they might think, "So what if this specialty requires me to go door-to-door asking strangers to buy my products? I actually hate that sort of thing, but I could probably grit my teeth and get through it anyway," simply to avoid letting go of a career dream they'd envisioned. Be honest with yourself about which career factors will be deal-killers for you. Saying "no" to one specialty allows you to continue your research to find a career that's a better overall fit.

Interview More Than One Person

You may interview a specialist on a day that is turning out to be horrible for him; his dog ate his car keys, he had to walk to the coffee shop to meet you, and he got mud on his pants along the way. By the time the two of you begin to talk, he could be in a wicked mood, and anything he tells you would be tainted by the circumstances of his grumpy morning. For this reason, it's important to interview *at least three people* in a particular career specialty before you make any concrete decisions. The minimum-of-three rule allows you to obtain a well-rounded picture of what a career would truly be like.

Make Adjustments in Your Focus Along the Way

Say that you conduct a career experiment to help you understand what it would be like to work as a pharmaceutical sales rep; you sit in the lobby of a busy medical clinic for an afternoon and observe the reps as they arrive and attempt to get an appointment with a decision maker at the office. After a few hours you notice that there's a lot of schlepping and rejection in that type of work. The reps haul in huge cases filled with their laptops and samples, and have to practically beg to get past the front desk. "Hmmm…" you think. "That looks a little too competitive for me. But still, I like the idea of outside sales. What kind of sales specialty would have less hustle and fewer rejections associated with it?" You review your Passion Zones and Career Ideas to Consider list and see Plant Sales Specialist.

What would it be like to sell interior and exterior plant services to large office buildings? Probably less cutthroat, so you decide to switch gears and look into that specialty for a while.

Just like the scientist who is continually adjusting her components to find the best formula, you will need to make several tweaks to your research to find the right career fit for you.

Persist Through Confusion

Herminia Ibarra, Ph.D., a career counselor and instructor at the Harvard School of Business, describes the career-change experiences of several adults in her book, *Working Identity*. After reading her book, I realized that my clients' career-change processes had been very similar to hers. Specifically, instead of following a direct point-A-to-point-B route, as in "Step 1: I want to change to a career as a designer of handbags. Step 2: I have changed careers and am now a handbag designer," people typically experience a process that follows a path more similar to point A to point M to point J and finally to point P.

As an example, a career changer's research process may go like this: "I think I want to be a designer of handbags." Then after gathering some career information this idea evolves to "I think I want to be a designer of hats" and then to "I think I want to be a sales representative for headwear," and finally to "I definitely want to be a sales representative for textiles." At the beginning of the process, the career changer couldn't have predicted that she would want to sell textiles, but after learning more about what was entailed in each career, her research path led her to making a choice that was ideal for her.

For this reason, *it's extremely important to be persistent throughout your field research process*. It can be helpful to tell yourself at the very beginning, "Most likely, I will need to research a number of career paths before I find one that is right for me. And chances are it will take me a few months to hone in on a career match that meets my criteria. Yet finding a good-fit career is a priority for me, so I will persist and not get discouraged."

Panic Point! Career Cowards often worry that they'll *never* find a career that's "just right" for them. This is a common fear. And for a while, especially in the first few months of your research, it may seem as if you're not getting any closer to your career-change goal. Yet if you persist, continuing to gather information and making necessary adjustments to your plan, you *will* uncover a career formula that's just right for you!

Remember That Change Can Be Messy

We've all had fantasies about how we'll be able to easily and almost *instantly* change a frustrating situation into a positive one. You know…the daydream where you're sitting at your desk doing your miserable job, and a terrific boss rides up on her white horse and whisks you away to a new career that you love.

Most of us would rather not concern ourselves with all of the little details involved in what it really takes to make a career change happen. We just want to wave a magic wand and have it completed! Yet in reality, we *know* that to make a major change in our lives requires executing lots of little steps. Although many of the steps will be enjoyable and energizing (because you'll be moving toward something you want), some of them will feel like drudgery and make you feel uncomfortable.

In *Transitions*, one of my all-time favorite keys-to-a-happy-life books, author William Bridges describes how when we go through a transition (such as changing careers), we typically experience three phases:

- **Endings,** where something we've been used to for a while is no longer the reality,

- **The Neutral Zone,** that middle step where things can seem confusing or chaotic for a while as you define your new plan, and

- **New Beginnings,** where life starts to fall into place and make sense again.

The very nature of defining a new career path throws you smack-dab into the Neutral Zone for a while, and most people (Career Cowards especially) hate it! They want to know the answer *right now*, without having to go through any anguish and confusion. But alas (sigh), things don't happen that way.

I find it's best to set yourself up for the expectation that for a while, things are going to be confusing. Also, tell yourself, "I may feel uncomfortable for a period of time, but this is normal, and if I persist, eventually I'll arrive at my own wonderful New Beginning."

Why It's Worth Doing

Think about how frustrated you are in your current career situation, and for how long you've felt this way. Day after day you've suffered through feeling as though your talents and skills aren't being used, doing work that feels meaningless to you. Worst of all, you're not being true to how you want to live your life. Pretty bad, huh?

Now think about some of the frustrations you're feeling as you research and define a better career path. Yes, parts of this process are confusing, but you *are* taking steps to make things better (even though they may be small steps, and it may feel as if you're taking two steps forward and one step back most of the time). You *are* making progress!

Finally, compare the pain of staying in your present career situation with the challenges you're facing with your career research. The first is an ongoing exercise of spinning your wheels in frustration, with little hope of making things better; the second is a period of short-term discomfort that if you persist through it, will lead to long-term career satisfaction. Is it worth it to push through the challenges to define a good-fit career path for yourself? You decide.

Career Champ Profile: Liselle

"I'm so frustrated!" Liselle complained to me in one of our weekly career-counseling sessions. "I thought for sure that working as a recruiter in an employment agency was what I wanted to do, but now I'm changing my mind. I just want to figure this out and move on!"

Liselle had been diligently conducting career experiments and interviewing specialists for almost three months, and she was anxious to make a decision. Her interest in working with people had first caused her to consider a career as a human resources generalist. Yet after interviewing three people in that profession, she decided to cross that idea off of her list. "Too much paperwork and too many rules to follow," Liselle explained to me.

She decided to redirect her focus to something in the human resources field that would require less paperwork and rules, and interviewed two people working as recruiters at employment agencies. Initially this specialty looked like a good match for Liselle; the work required fewer rules and paperwork. Plus she liked how the recruiters described their work as being fast paced and varied.

To further confirm that recruiting would be a good choice for her, Liselle arranged to job-shadow a specialist at a local employment service. For three hours one Monday afternoon, she sat in a chair watching the action in the agency. We met the next day…the day Liselle was feeling so frustrated.

"I didn't like what I saw," Liselle explained. "The recruiters in that office are constantly fighting fires, trying to put the right candidates in the right jobs as quickly as possible. Plus they rarely ever leave their seats. They stare at computers and are on the phone most of the day. I like to move around! Will I ever, *ever* find a new career that fits me well?"

I then told Liselle that typically, most Career Cowards discover that their first few career-change ideas won't work out, and that this is *very normal.* "That's why it was so important to create those long lists of Passion Zones and Career Areas to Consider. If one idea doesn't work out, you still have several more possibilities to check into."

Reluctantly, Liselle agreed to look at her lists again. "Well, there is the idea of professional organizer—you know, someone who helps people with homes or offices that are really cluttered to make those spaces more pleasant and efficient," she offered. "I've always liked that idea, but never really thought I could do it. But it wouldn't hurt to at least explore it through some career experiments and informational interviews, would it?" Still anxious to make her career-change decision—but not wanting to make a fast choice that would turn out to be the wrong one—Liselle agreed to persist with some additional field research.

Just a month later, Liselle had made her career-change decision. After interviewing a number of professional organizers, Liselle discovered the specialty would allow her to work with people and provide her the variety she liked, plus she'd get to move around quite a bit in her work.

Once she decided to pursue that path, Liselle reconnected with people she'd interviewed to ask for ideas and referrals. Saul, the owner of a closet-design business, offered Liselle a job as an assistant. Liselle's new career was launched!

Core Courage Concept

It takes courage and persistence to keep trying when you run into a roadblock or discover disappointing information. You may begin to think, "Wouldn't it be easier if I just sucked it up and stayed in the career I'm doing now?" Yet you know over the long term, you'd be frustrated and unhappy. Although gathering career-change information can be challenging and confusing, it *is* a process that inch by inch, step by step, is taking you toward your goals. You can do it, and you *will* persist through it, because you know it's a worthwhile investment in yourself.

Confidence Checklist

- ☐ Make a pros and cons list.
- ☐ Refer to your prioritized list of values often.
- ☐ Be honest with yourself.
- ☐ Interview more than one person.
- ☐ Make adjustments in your focus along the way.
- ☐ Persist through confusion.
- ☐ Remember that change can be messy.

Chapter 11

Handle Career-Change Confusion

Feeling confused? Running into barriers? Not sure how to work around a career-change challenge you've encountered? Whether it's a problem with making enough income, gaining the training you need, or deciding among several interesting possibilities, this chapter presents proven strategies that can help you break through your dilemma and keep moving forward.

Risk It or Run From It?

- **Risk Rating:** Low to moderate (you're beginning to make some concrete decisions now).

- **Payoff Potential:** Really, really great! Troubleshooting career-change challenges now will allow you to achieve the career lifestyle you desire.

- **Time to Complete:** A few minutes of planning time…or up to a few years of training and development, depending on what you choose to do.

- **Bailout Strategy:** Again, if you're certain of your career-change strategy, move on to the next chapter (although there

(continued)

(continued)

are some pretty cool ideas in here that you may want to consider).

- **The "20 Percent Extra" Edge:** Putting in the time now to create a solid career-change plan can save you years of wasted time and energy.

- **"Go For It!" Bonus Activity:** Go back to the ideal career vision you created in chapter 2 and review what you wrote. Add in any new details you've discovered and consider how the ideas presented in this chapter might fit into your overall plan.

How to Push Through Uncertainty to Create a Clearer Career-Change Plan

Right now you're at the part of the career-change process that typically feels most confusing for Career Cowards. It could be compared to standing in the vortex of a tornado, watching thousands of things swirl by, not being able to see anything very clearly, and feeling very hesitant to take a step in any particular direction. Although it may feel uncomfortable, the confusion you're encountering is a necessary part of the process. The following concepts should help clarify some of what might be perplexing to you now.

Troubleshoot Unrealistic Career-Change Options

Sometimes, especially in the early stages of research, Career Cowards discover that what they'd imagined about a new career turns out to be unrealistic. Either the specialty doesn't exist or won't fit their lifestyle needs. This can be extremely disappointing and is enough to send some people running back to the safe haven of their current (yet miserable) occupations. However, after observing the successes of hundreds of career changers, I've discovered that although your initial research may yield disappointing results, if you persist in your pursuit of the right fit, new, more realistic options will soon become apparent.

Panic Point! Have you learned that your initial career-change options won't work? Although that's frustrating (and probably a little scary), it's actually pretty normal to discover that there are problems with your first-round ideas. View this experience as an opportunity to keep gathering information so that, ultimately, you'll create a better overall career-change strategy *that succeeds.*

Remember, your goal is to find a career that offers what you want and need. It may take a while to discover the right solution for you, and you may have to change the course of your research a few times—but that's okay. Aim to view every piece of information you collect as a piece of the puzzle to your ultimate career solution. For a while, the image on the puzzle may be blurry, but hang in there until it becomes clear.

Work Around Career Possibilities That Don't Offer Enough Pay

"I love the idea of this new career, but the pay is terrible!" This is a frequent frustration of career changers who are drawn to creative or entrepreneurial careers. If your desired occupation won't pay enough, should you even consider pursuing it? Before making any final decisions about a career possibility based on its income potential, answer the following:

- How do professionals in that field make it work for them? Do they have multiple occupations? Expand their work into related areas to generate more income? For instance, one of my neighbors is a potter. In addition to making and selling beautiful wares, he teaches pottery-making lessons.

- What is the likelihood that you could eventually earn enough income, within a reasonable period of time? Most startup businesses take about two years to begin generating a profit. Would you be able to wait out that ramp-up period? Another consideration is that the majority of startup businesses fail.

If yours turns out to be unsuccessful, what would be your backup plan?

One of the most successful options for Career Cowards who are drawn to a low-paying career path is to combine it with another, more lucrative specialty. Although you may end up getting to pursue your passion only part time, having a slice of career satisfaction is better than none at all! Plus, over time you may discover ways to grow your passion into full-time work.

Panic Point! "Oh, no!" you may worry, "I'll need to take a significant pay cut to get into the career field I want!" This is a common problem for Career Cowards who discover that they need to take several steps backward in responsibility and income in order to get started in their desired career area. Some successful career changers have worked around this problem by cutting their expenses to the new-career income level *before* they make the change (and banking the money they save), to prove to themselves they're able to survive on that level of pay. Also keep in mind that the skills you've gained in your former career will help you progress faster than someone with less experience and allow you to earn better pay more quickly than the average worker in your new career field.

Address the "Need More Training" Requirement

A lack of a certification or degree can be a maddening roadblock for career changers, especially if you've defined a career path that excites you, yet you can't move into it because you don't possess the right kind of training. Rather than throw away an excellent career possibility, consider these avenues to work around or through a lack-of-training barrier:

- **Begin at the bottom.** Although you may at first resist the idea of taking steps backward in pay or responsibility, beginning in an entry-level position makes it easier for you to get started in your chosen career field. Once you're in, you will then be more likely to discover avenues to obtain the training you need, and may even be able to have your employer pay for it.

- **Aim for a position that requires less training.** If you're interested in becoming a physical therapist, for instance, and don't want to complete several years of college to get your degree, you could become a physical therapy technician instead. Frequently technicians can be trained on-the-job or with just a year or two of formal instruction.

- **Bite the bullet and get the training.** When I decided to become a career counselor, I at first resisted the idea of getting a masters degree. It would take me two years and cost me thousands of dollars. But then I thought about what I would gain from it: credibility and the qualifications I would need to pursue the kind of work I sincerely wanted to do. Once I decided to go for it, a huge wave of relief washed over me. Even though I was still scared about the time and financial commitment involved, I could see that I'd be able to accomplish what I truly wanted in my career. And as it turned out, getting the degree was one of the most fun and rewarding experiences in my life — even though I wound up with some pretty hefty student loans in the process.

Decide Between Two or More Appealing Careers

Let's say that you've identified more than one career-change option that you love. Do you really have to choose one over the other? Maybe not! Consider these possibilities for taking advantage of multiple career-change opportunities:

- **Create a "muffin tin" career.** Typically, when you think of having a career, you imagine it to be a single profession that you immerse yourself in and develop over time. Another possibility is to select more than one career and to execute them simultaneously. So, instead of developing a single "loaf" of a career, you might create several smaller "muffins."

For instance, imagine that you love the idea of having a career as a personal chef, preparing weekly meals for multiple clients. Yet you also love the idea of writing children's books, as well as creating Web sites for small businesses. Instead of choosing just one of these specialties, you could do them all! Muffin tin careers are especially well suited for Career Cowards who like a lot of variety and are great multitaskers.

- **Become a serial careerist.** Are you drawn to so many interesting career options that you'd like to live several lifetimes just to have the chance to experience them all? Although the "multiple lifetimes" opportunity may be iffy, you do have the option to become involved in numerous professions over the course of your time on this planet. And if the muffin tin approach seems too scattered for your tastes, think about the possibility of becoming involved in multiple careers over several years.

  You could work as a paralegal for five years, for example, and then move on to work as an emergency medical technician for the next five, and then evolve that into a career as an investment broker. There's no rule that says you have to stick with one specialty for your entire working life.

Almost *always*, when you run into a roadblock in your career-change planning, a workaround option exists if you're willing to persist in finding it.

Realize That It's Okay Not to Make a Career Change After All

Sometimes, after gathering information about different careers, Career Cowards discover that their current work really isn't so bad after all. Perhaps, for instance, you *thought* that moving into a particular career would bring you greater satisfaction, yet when you researched it you learned that it wasn't really what you expected. Now your present career specialty seems more appealing than before.

Observing the experiences of my clients over the last several years, I've discovered that about 20 percent of Career Cowards eventually arrive at the "Maybe my current career's not so bad after all" realization. *It's perfectly fine to come to this conclusion.* Double-check that you're truly choosing it because it's the right fit for you by putting it to the decision test in the next chapter.

Why It's Worth Doing

A one-size career does not fit all. Everyone has special needs and hopes, so your aim is to find the right combination of factors to address *your* lifestyle, interests, and talent requirements. It may take a while to discover the right formula, but never lose sight of what you aim to create for yourself: a career that brings you greater levels of satisfaction and success. A bit of persistence now will pay off hugely later on.

Career Champ Profile: Wyatt

For several years, Wyatt taught Spanish at a local college. Although he loved using his language skills, he longed to get involved in work that would allow him to spend more time outdoors, riding his bike and seeing more of the world. His skills, talents, and interests initially pointed him in the direction of experiential instructor working at a university, where he would take groups of students on trips to Spanish-speaking countries. Wyatt also spoke Portuguese and sign language, additional skills that would be useful in that line of work.

Yet after he interviewed a few experiential instructors about their careers, he discovered that because it was such an appealing position to so many people, jobs were highly competitive and offered very low pay. Wyatt decided to set aside the idea of becoming an experiential instructor for a while, and to investigate other careers instead.

For the next four months, Wyatt interviewed more than 40 people working in a range of outdoor- and language-oriented specialties.

Then one day he walked into my office with a huge smile on his face. "I've figured it out!" he said. "Rather than one career, I'm going to have three!" He then went on to describe how, after interviewing so many specialists, he'd finally discovered how he could have the lifestyle he wanted while doing work that he loved.

"Part of my work will involve taking groups of travelers to Spanish-speaking countries on cycling tours," Wyatt began, describing how tour companies would contract with people with Wyatt's background to lead travelers through international locales. "I'm also going to start a hammock-sales business. Through my travels to South America, I've located suppliers who make beautiful hammocks that I can sell on a Web site and through kiosks in high-traffic shopping areas." I told Wyatt that I thought his plan sounded brilliant so far.

"Well, there's more," he continued. His eyes twinkled and his snow-white beard bobbed as he explained the final piece of his career strategy. "In the process of interviewing all of those people, someone suggested that I consider becoming a natural Santa Claus, working at upscale malls during the holiday season. My Spanish and sign-language skills are especially marketable in major metropolitan areas. In fact, I discovered that I can land Santa jobs that will pay as much as $20,000 for just two months' work!"

As it turned out, Wyatt did go on to implement his plan, and years later, he's still actively involved in his three-part career, doing work that brings him joy while also meeting his lifestyle needs.

Core Courage Concept

Ultimately, you want to create a career you love. Although you may wish it would come together with no complications or difficulties, your practical side understands that with every great result, some struggle is involved. Rather than throw in the towel at the first sign of difficulty or fear, why not admit to yourself that you're confused and scared, and choose to push through it to create a better situation for yourself? Although the answer may be fuzzy for a long time, eventually—if you persist—your career future will come clear…and you will have developed newfound strength and courage along the way.

Confidence Checklist

☐ Troubleshoot unrealistic career-change options.

☐ Work around career possibilities that don't offer enough pay.

☐ Address the "need more training" requirement.

☐ Decide between two or more appealing careers.

☐ Realize that it's okay not to make a career change after all.

Make the Right Choice for You

You know when you're getting close to finding what you want. Like a hound dog sniffing out a raccoon, your instincts practically scream, "You're going the right way!" when you find a good trail. When this happens, try not to second-guess yourself or overanalyze what's happening. Although it may feel overwhelming, just keep taking deep breaths and keep putting one foot in front of the other. You're headed to an exciting place!

Risk It or Run From It?

- **Risk Rating:** Pretty significant; you're about to make a career-choice decision. But remember…you still have a number of steps to complete and can make course corrections as necessary.

- **Payoff Potential:** Fantastic! Your brighter, happier career future is just around the corner.

- **Time to Complete:** An hour or so (or a few more weeks if you decide you need to go back a step or two to gather some additional information).

(continued)

(continued)

- **Bailout Strategy:** Already crystal-clear about your career-change choice? Feel free to move on to the next chapter.

- **The "20 Percent Extra" Edge:** So far, you've done your homework and thought things through carefully. As a result, the choices you make here will most likely be solid rather than reactionary.

- **"Go For It!" Bonus Activity:** In addition to filling out the Career-Change Decision Worksheet, review your Talents and Skills, Passion Zones, and Values lists carefully to identify opportunities for further refinement of your career-change choice to make it an even better fit for you.

How to Analyze Your Career Data and Make a Successful Choice

Over the last several weeks, you've diligently collected career information through experiments and informational interviews. You've persisted through the frustration of bumping into roadblocks and redefining your plan. But now a career picture is starting to emerge. Take the final step toward confirming your career-change decision with the following activities.

Put Your Career-Change Choice to the Test

You're homing in on a career-change decision. How does your selection fit with the Skills, Talents, Passion Zones, and Values you defined earlier in this book? Do you truly know enough about the career path you're considering to make a decision? Fill in the following Career-Change Decision Worksheet to see how your potential choice stacks up.

Career-Change Decision Worksheet

Career Specialty You're Considering:_____

Career Factor	Doesn't Fit	Fits a Little	Decent Fit	Excellent Fit!

Top Skills and Talents Used in This Career:

Skill/Talent 1: _____ _____ _____ _____

Skill/Talent 2: _____ _____ _____ _____

Skill/Talent 3: _____ _____ _____ _____

Skill/Talent 4: _____ _____ _____ _____

Skill/Talent 5: _____ _____ _____ _____

Passion Zone(s) Involved in This Career:

Passion
Zone 1: _____ _____ _____ _____

Passion
Zone 2: _____ _____ _____ _____

Passion
Zone 3: _____ _____ _____ _____

Lifestyle Values Required for This Career:

Value 1: _____ _____ _____ _____

Value 2: _____ _____ _____ _____

Value 3: _____ _____ _____ _____

Value 4: _____ _____ _____ _____

Value 5: _____ _____ _____ _____

(continued)

(continued)

Key Decision Questions:

- Which of my significant Skills or Talents would I *not* be able to use if I pursued this career path?_____

  _____

  _____

- Which Passion Zones important to me would *not* be involved this career choice?_____

  _____

  _____

- Which of my Values would *not* be honored with this career decision?_____

  _____

  _____

- How will I be impacted, short term and long term, by the factors that will *not* be addressed in this career choice?_____

  _____

  _____

- How does this choice align with my Ideal Career vision?_____

  _____

  _____

Well, how did your career-change decision perform? Sometimes as Career Cowards try to fill in the worksheet, they realize they don't know the answers to some of the questions. If this happens to you, revisit the activities in chapters 6, 7, and 8 to gather the information you need.

Or maybe you discovered that there are elements of your career choice that just won't work for your needs. If that's the case, you have every right to be disappointed, yet *please don't give up!* Review the career options list you created in chapter 4 and pick some new ideas to investigate. Although right now you may feel as if you'll *never* find a good fit, it's highly likely that an excellent career-change option is right around the corner for you—if you persist to find it.

Or did your career-change idea pass with flying colors? If so, congratulations! You're about to embark on the next exciting phase of your career-change process. Read on!

Panic Point! As you focus in on a career change choice, Career Cowards often begin to worry, "What if I choose the wrong thing? What if, even though this *seems* to be a good choice for me, ultimately it turns out to be a mistake?" Keep in mind that as you continue to move forward, you'll still be taking small, safe steps—not huge, scary leaps. If you discover that a step forward is the wrong move for you, you can backtrack and try another approach. Remember also that if you choose to move forward on a new career path, and then change your mind, *you can almost always go back to your former career.* The career-change choice you make now is not a life sentence! You can continue to modify and evolve your strategy over time to make it fit your needs and goals.

Understand the Steps Involved with Implementing Your Plan

Now that you've decided which path to pursue for your career change, you'll now move into the execution phase of your process. In the following chapters, you'll discover how to

- Gain experience to get started in your new career, through internships, self study, on-the-job training, or a formal study program.

- Create a resume that highlights your skills as they relate to your new career path.

- Find work in your new specialty, including locating and presenting yourself to potential employers.

- Build expertise in your new career, from learning the basics to developing a solid foundation for future career successes.

As you can see, there are many steps still ahead of you in this career-change process. Although you may feel a little overwhelmed right now, have faith in yourself; you've come a long way already, and you *will* be able to complete the journey successfully.

Why It's Worth Doing

At some point, you *have* to put a stake in the ground and say to yourself, "Even though it may scare me to do it, I need to decide on a career-change goal and move forward." If you don't make a decision, you risk wasting years of your life—as well as living in frustration. If your career choice fared well on the Career-Change Decision Worksheet, take a deep breath and *go for it!*

Career Champ Profile: Dolores

For years, Dolores struggled day after day in her job as a graphic designer, working for a landscape architecture firm. Even though the job allowed her to use graphics tools, it didn't allow for much creativity; her boss told her exactly how to design each project, and Dolores's artistic talents were pleading to be applied in her work.

In an attempt to find a better fit, Dolores used the exercises described in this book to combine her talents, skills, and passion zones, and created an exciting list of career possibilities. She then dove into an intense period of career experiments and informational interviews to determine which choice would be right for her. Along the way, she investigated becoming a personal trainer (addressing her strong interest in fitness), a chef (another highly creative specialty), and a Web programmer for Web design companies.

Over time, the career option that percolated to the top was running her own Web design company. When Dolores tested her idea against the Career-Change Decision Worksheet, the biggest concern was the possibility that for two years or longer, she might not make any income, plus she and her husband would need to sink money into the business to get it started. "But my husband and I have been good about saving money, and we have enough set aside to get this business started and to live for a few years," she reasoned.

Even though it made her nervous to do it, Dolores decided to move forward on her career-change plan. Over the next few months, she launched her business and was actually able to make a profit in the first year of operation. Best of all, she was wildly happy in her new career!

Core Courage Concept

Wow, you're making a *decision* regarding which career-change option to implement. How scary…and exciting! But before you get let yourself get too overwhelmed, remember all the steps you've taken so far (and succeeded with), and have faith that as you encounter the next challenges, you'll be able to succeed. Typically, deciding which career option to choose is the most difficult step for Career Cowards, yet *implementing* that choice is usually fun and energizing. So congrats, you've already made it through what will probably be the hardest part for you. Now on to the truly exciting part: making your career change dream a reality!

Confidence Checklist

☐ Put your career-change choice to the test.

☐ Understand the steps involved with implementing your plan.

Part 4

Transition to a New Career Painlessly

Chapter 13

Build a Bridge to Your New Career

You've decided on your future career path; now you're going to make it happen! Through the energizing, experience-building activities described in this chapter, you'll be able to build an effective bridge into your new career. Internships, self-study activities, on-the-job training, and formal study programs can all help you successfully progress into your new work.

Risk It or Run From It?

- **Risk Rating:** A little higher now, because you're taking some definite steps forward (but you're nowhere near "run away screaming!" risks yet).

- **Payoff Potential:** Phenomenal! You're about to make your career-change dreams a reality. Just imagine the satisfaction you'll feel as you achieve your career goals.

- **Time to Complete:** A few days or weeks to a few years (but don't panic...you're bound to enjoy the time you invest).

- **Bailout Strategy:** You could attempt to jump into your new career cold turkey, with no bridge-building experiences

(continued)

(continued)

> under your belt. You may be able to pull it off (especially if you have connections in the right places and are very good at selling yourself). Skip to the next chapter if bridge-building just isn't for you.
>
> - **The "20 Percent Extra" Edge:** Once again, most career-change wannabes only think about making their career goals happen—and never make much progress. Executing the activities in this chapter will effectively move you out of the thinking phase into the achieving-your-goals phase.
>
> - **"Go For It!" Bonus Activity:** Create a detailed menu of potential bridge experiences, providing yourself with several options to consider and implement over time.

How to Transition into Your New Career

You're excited! You've selected a new career path. Now you'll gain valuable experience to convince yourself (as well as future employers) that you've got what it takes to succeed in your new career.

Take an Inventory of Your Transferable Experience

Most likely, a good deal of the experience you've acquired in your life can be put to use in your new specialty. Your challenge is to identify which of those skills apply, and then to translate them into relevant descriptions for use on your resume and in interviews.

To begin this process, refer to the Career-Change Decision Worksheet you completed in chapter 12 and remind yourself of the skills and talents most important for your chosen career. Then ask yourself, "When in my life have I demonstrated my ability in these areas?" Your examples may come from both professional and personal experiences.

Often, it's helpful to review your existing resume, performance reviews, school transcripts, and other records of your experiences to remind yourself of your skills and accomplishments. Create as long of a list as you can, writing down every example you can recall. Later, you'll select which experiences are most relevant.

If you struggle with identifying skills and experiences that may be transferable, refer to the detailed, step-by-step exercises included in my first book, *The Career Coward's Guide to Interviewing,* for additional ideas and guidance.

Consider Formal Training to Fill in the Gaps

After you've taken an inventory of your current experience and background, you may determine that you've got some holes to fill. At first this may feel overwhelming to a Career Coward. "Will I be able to get the training I need, as well as succeed with the new skills?" you might wonder. From where you're standing now, it may seem like a terribly long road to arrive at the point where you're actually doing the work you love. But keep in mind that

a. You've already learned and succeeded with *many* things in your life—and you'll be able to succeed with this, too, and

b. Even if you decide to pursue additional training, you'll be learning about something that jazzes and motivates you!

The information you acquire will move you toward something that interests and energizes you; the learning part of the process will be fun, rather than a drudge.

Panic Point! Are you panicking, thinking, "Oh no! To do the work I want to do will require me to get more training. Can I afford it? Make the time? Succeed with the course-work?" Although this step may feel overwhelming at first, remember: New skills are acquired one tiny step at a time. Rather than get yourself all worked up, break it down into smaller steps. Which classes would you actually need to take? Where would you get trained? Chances are, once you analyze the smaller steps, they'll feel more doable (and even exciting) to you.

So how do you determine whether you need formal training? Some positions absolutely require a degree or certification for you to be able to engage in them legally. Take architecture, for example. Because lives depend on an architect's ability to build safe, sound structures, they must pass certification exams to become a licensed architect. With that profession, there would be no way to sidestep formal training and licensing.

With *most* professions, however, formal training is optional, and you could potentially enter a new career field without an additional degree or certification. You can determine whether formal training is necessary for your new career by answering the following questions:

- Is a specific license or certification required to enter this field?

- Of the specialists I interviewed, what kind of training did they have?

- When I look at sample job descriptions, what kind of training do the ads most often include?

- Are there avenues, other than formal training, through which I can gain the training I need?

- Based on my track record so far, how do I best learn? Is it through self-study or in a more structured training program?

If you do decide that formal training makes the most sense for you, take the time to locate a respected training source that will truly deliver what you need. Before committing to any training curriculum, talk with specialists in your chosen career field, as well as with former students of the program you're considering, for input and recommendations.

Use Self-Study to Move Ahead

Often it's possible to plug gaps in your background through experiences you gain on your own. For instance, say that you've decided to transition into a career as a public relations specialist working for a marketing agency. This specialty would allow you to easily build expertise by reading books about public relations, studying the work of other public relations specialists, and developing a portfolio of your work, using actual or hypothetical subjects in your examples.

The career experiments and practice projects described in chapter 6 offer several ideas for self-study and skill building. You can also ask the specialists you interviewed for self-study suggestions, as well as for practice projects that you can execute under their guidance.

Line up an Internship or Work-for-Free Opportunity

Internships have been around for decades, providing an avenue for someone with little to no experience to gain know-how in a new career. They range from highly structured programs, organized and monitored through learning institutions, to informal agreements between the expert and the novice. Interns sometimes earn pay for their efforts, but most often they work for free in exchange for the opportunity to learn a new trade.

Panic Point! You may be thinking, "What? Me, work for free? No way! I need to make money!" This is a common Career Coward reaction, especially if you've never been involved in an internship before. At first, the concept of devoting your time and talents for no monetary reward may seem ridiculous. Yet consider this: An unpaid internship is similar to a training program. Only instead of paying a school with a check or credit card, you're investing your time and effort in exchange for training. Overall, working for free may be perhaps the most cost-effective new-career avenue you can take!

If you're enrolled in a formal training program, your school may be able to help you line up an internship. Or you may need to seek out and arrange your own opportunity. Either way, the following guidelines will help you structure a win-win experience for both you and the employer:

- **Create a detailed list of what you want to learn.** Refer to your informational interview notes and sample job descriptions to determine which of your skills need the most development. Be specific about what you want to learn; it will help the employer arrange opportunities that deliver the experiences you seek.

- **Also develop a list of ways you can benefit the employer.** You may be thinking, "Some employer is going to be so lucky to have me interning for her—especially if I work for free!" Although there are benefits to employers for having interns around, in general, the effort required to successfully manage an intern outweighs any benefit received. Although you may be enthusiastic and talented, an employer will still need to invest time and resources to get you to a point where you're trained and productive. For this reason, it's helpful to articulate ways in which you can benefit an employer. Review your inventory of transferable experience for ideas. Brainstorming with potential employers about your internship will also help you define ways in which you can benefit them.

- **Determine a mutually agreeable work arrangement.** It's easiest if an employer knows exactly when you'll be around. Devoting 10 to 20 hours per week, over a period of two to four months, is usually a sufficient timeframe.

- **Target potential internship sites and present your proposal.** Through your informational interview and career experiment activities, you've probably already identified a few organizations involved in the kind of work you want to do. You might even want to reconnect with your informational interview contacts as potential sources for your internship. See chapter 15 for additional ideas on identifying potential employers. Once you've created your list of target sites, contact them with a letter similar to the one in figure 13.1, mailed along with your "What I hope to learn" and "How I can benefit your organization" lists.

Dear [NAME],

Recently I made the decision to transition into a career in [SPECIALTY]. I have researched this specialty carefully and find it to be a good match with my talents and interests.

I am now seeking an opportunity to learn some basic skills in [SPECIALTY] through an internship, potentially with your organization.

Toward this goal, I have attached a preliminary list of the specific skills in which I hope to gain experience, as well as a list of skills I already possess that may be of benefit to your organization. My hope would be to arrange an internship where I could devote between 10 to 20 hours each week, over a period of two to three months. I do not expect to be paid for this opportunity.

Would you be willing to meet with me to discuss the possibility of me conducting an internship with your organization? In the next few days, I will follow up with you to confirm receipt of this proposal and to determine a logical next step. Thank you in advance for your consideration of my request.

Sincerely,

[YOUR NAME]

Figure 13.1: Sample internship proposal letter.

For additional guidance on how to best present yourself in this meeting, refer to the step-by-step how-to's described in *The Career Coward's Guide to Interviewing*.

Land a Part-Time Job

Similar to an internship, a part-time job may be the ideal avenue to help you bridge into your new career. Working evenings or weekends would allow you to keep your day job while building expertise in your new career. Keep in mind that most jobs aren't advertised. If you have an idea about a part-time job that would help you gain the experience you want, don't wait for the position to show up in the newspaper. Rather, contact the potential employer directly to ask about possibilities.

Why It's Worth Doing

Although you can attempt to dive into your new career based solely on your current skills and experience, you will most likely run into roadblocks with potential employers. "You don't have any relevant background," they may argue. "Why should I hire you when I can hire someone who already knows the ropes?"

For this reason, gaining new skills through self-study, formal training, internship, or part-time work builds your credibility in the eyes of a potential employer and boosts your confidence in yourself. Sure, it will take some time, effort, and maybe money to learn some new skills, but keep in mind that these activities are an investment in yourself, moving you steadily toward your desired career-change goals.

Career Champ Profile: Bryce

After working for more than 20 years as a manager at a utilities company, Bryce decided to switch careers into something more interesting to him. Although he was skeptical about what an experienced utilities manager could really accomplish with a career change, he plodded through the assessment exercises to create a Career Specialties to Consider list of 20 intriguing possibilities and then interviewed specialists in several careers about their work.

To his delight and surprise, Bryce's career research led him to a specialty that seemed both interesting and attainable: private investigator. Bryce interviewed three PIs; determined that the work would be an excellent fit for his talents, skills, and interests; and ultimately decided to take the plunge and make a change.

Because working as a PI requires no formal training, Bryce decided to work for free to gain some basic knowledge. Bryce developed an internship proposal, offering to assist an established PI in his work—without being paid—in exchange for getting trained on some basic PI procedures. The proposal specified that Bryce would work up to 20 hours each week, with 10 hours being devoted to whatever the experienced PI wanted him to do (filing, paperwork, scrubbing toilets, you name it), and 10 hours dedicated to learning essential PI practices.

Bryce presented his proposal to six successful PI firms before he found one that agreed to take him on. Yet the owner of the firm didn't want Bryce to work for free. Instead, he offered to pay Bryce a fair rate. Bryce began working immediately. Years later, Bryce is now a successful PI, earning competitive pay doing work that he loves!

Core Courage Concept

It's already taken a lot of courage to define a career-change goal for yourself. Now you're faced with the challenge of taking things further and actually bridging into your new work. This may seem especially scary…what if you fail? Yet keep in mind that *bridge experiences are designed to help you learn*. You're bound to flounder and make mistakes. When you falter and begin to lose confidence, take a deep breath and remind yourself that you're still learning, and that ultimately your goal is to move into work that you love. In the end, you'll learn what you need to know and ultimately succeed!

Confidence Checklist

☐ Take an inventory of your transferable experience.

☐ Consider formal training to fill in gaps.

☐ Use self-study to move ahead.

☐ Line up an internship or work-for-free opportunity.

☐ Land a part-time job.

Chapter 14

Create a New-You Resume for Your New Career

You're making great progress toward realizing your career-change goals: You've defined your new career path and have begun acquiring relevant experience. To take things to the next step, now it's time to describe what you have to offer on a resume. "Can I persuade an employer that I can cut it in this new career?" you may be worrying. Developing a strong career-change resume will help you see that that yes, you can!

Risk It or Run From It?

- **Risk Rating:** Low. You're just getting prepared to present the new you to prospective employers through your resume.

- **Payoff Potential:** Substantial. How you present yourself on your resume can make the difference between being taken seriously and not being considered at all.

- **Time to Complete:** A few hours.

- **Bailout Strategy:** You can use your old resume and hope that an employer will be able to read between the lines about how your background applies to your new specialty.

(continued)

(continued)

> But since you have only one chance to make a successful, new-you impression, why not put a little time into making your resume as effective as it can be?
>
> - **The "20 Percent Extra" Edge:** Taking the time now to build a solid resume that highlights what you have to offer makes for a much smoother transition down the line.
>
> - **"Go For It!" Bonus Activity:** Think about the people you know who have successfully changed careers. Ask to see their career-change resumes for ideas. And check out other examples online and in resume books (for example, *Expert Resumes for Career Changers*).

How to Paint a Convincing Picture of the "New You" in Your Resume

You've decided on your new career path and have gained some relevant experience in your new specialty through career experiments and bridge experiences. Now you have the opportunity to paint a brand-new picture of what you have to offer. The following career-change tips for resumes will have both you and future employers clearly seeing your potential.

Build a Strong Foundation with a List of Keywords

Just as you need something solid to build the foundation of a house (bricks, concrete, stones, and so on), you'll want to build your resume on a solid foundation. Keywords—the words and phrases used to describe the core functions of your new career—provide you that solid, effective base for your resume. Plus they're easy to compile, even for Career Cowards!

Begin by locating three to five job descriptions that match the kind of position you hope to land. A job search site such as www.monster.com is a great place to look. Simply plug in the job title for the kind of position you're aiming for, such as "Meeting

Planner," and review the job descriptions that the search engine provides. Don't worry about the geographic location of the positions. You won't necessarily be applying to these jobs; you're just interested in the keywords used in the job descriptions.

For instance, I located the following keywords from three Meeting Planner descriptions I reviewed:

- Responsible for all aspects of planning, coordinating, communicating, and executing meetings and events.

- 25 to 50 percent travel, which may include overnight stays.

- Hotel selection, budget preparation, contract negotiations, selection of food/beverage and audio visual equipment.

- Evaluate and negotiate vendors for both on-site and off-site events with the objective of a successful event as well as maximizing return on investment.

- Keep current on trends and changes within the industry to improve effectiveness as a planner and the overall success of corporate events.

- Bachelor's degree with a minimum of three years of experience in meeting planning in either a corporate setting or hotel/catering atmosphere.

- Strong organizational skills with the ability to handle multiple tasks and priorities under tight deadlines and budgets.

- Great customer service/communication skills, detail oriented and a self starter.

- Ensure all meeting materials are complete and accurate.

- Work closely with other team members to ensure successful execution of meeting.

Phrases like "planning, coordinating, and communicating; hotel selection, budget preparation, and contract negotiations" describe core responsibilities for meeting planners.

As you review the sample job descriptions you find, begin to build a list of the keywords—the longer the list, the better. After you've created a comprehensive list, review it and delete all the skills that don't pertain to your background. *If you've ever used a particular skill—even if it was for a practice project—it counts!* Err on the side of keeping as many relevant skills on your list as you can. You can use this edited list of key skills in a Relevant Skills section on your resume.

Pick the Best Resume Format for Your Needs

You probably already know that resumes can be developed in a variety of formats. Some of the most popular are *chronological,* which highlights your work history in order of time (with most recent experience first); *functional* (sometimes also called *skills-based*), which focuses on key skills in your background; and *hybrid,* which is a combination of both the chronological and functional formats.

For career changers like you, functional and hybrid formats are almost always the best choices because they allow you to call attention to the parts of your background that are most transferable and relevant to your new career.

An example of a functional resume format is included in the Career Champ section of this chapter, and figure 14.1 is an example of a hybrid resume format.

As you can see, skills are the main focus of this format. Similarly, as you create your career-change resume, you'll want to focus on three to five key skill areas that are most essential to your new position. To pick the most important areas, refer to the keywords list you created, as well as what you learned from specialists through your informational interviews.

Which three to five skill areas should you choose? It can be difficult to prioritize just a few as being most important. To decide, ask yourself, "Which skills would I be using *most* in my new career?" Although you won't have the chance to emphasize *every* relevant skill in your resume, you will be able to focus on the most important ones.

CHRIS WHITE, CPP   *HR Business Analyst / Payroll*
33 Wonderful Drive
Fort Collins, CO 80521
(970) 424-1111, chriswhite@hotmail.com

Capable Human Resources–Information Systems (HRIS) professional with expertise in information systems and payroll operations. Proven abilities as a technical leader for implementation of multiple Oracle support modules to support process improvement. Awarded highest recognition for outstanding attention to reporting conformance practices.

WORK HISTORY

BIG BUSINESS ORGANIZATION   2001–Present

Accounting Department Manager: *Oversee three payroll specialists and serve as department liaison for Human Resources implementation of Oracle information system modules.*

Payroll Department Management and Oversight:
- Control all systems to accomplish quality, on-time payroll processing for 2,000 employees.
- Supervise three full-time payroll team members, providing training, day-to-day direction, performance feedback, and employee-development guidance.
- Possess in-depth knowledge of organization's business, policy, and statutory requirements.
- Gather, refine, and document business requirements; perform workflow analyses and cost/benefit studies; research options to support complete solutions for the department.

Project Lead Liaison for Oracle Modules Implementation:
- Work with staff to assess needs, configure applications, provide information and assistance, develop procedures, troubleshoot simple and complex problems, satisfy expectations, and share knowledge on newly implemented Oracle modules.
  - ➤ *Example:* Worked with HR team to define, troubleshoot, and successfully implement Oracle OSB, OTL, HR, and Payroll modules. Maintained a productive and respectful working relationship with all parties during a stressful launch period.
- Apply technical expertise to support successful HRIS operations:
  - ➤ *Specific expertise:* MS Windows Vista, MS Office Suite, GroupWise E-mail, Data modeling software, Project Management Software, Internet Explorer, MS Access, Oracle Reports, Data Cube Tools (DynamiCube), as well as other current business applications in use within the department.

BIG COUNTY ORGANIZATION   1997–2001

Senior Accountant / Accounting Functions Supervisor
Performed day-to-day accounting functions and return-on-investment analyses, and presented financial reports and recommendations to Advisory Boards.

Additional work experiences in Bookkeeping and Accounting. Details provided on request.

EDUCATION & AFFILIATIONS
- B.S. Accounting, University of Colorado, 3.5 GPA
- A.A.S. Accounting, Aims Community College, 3.83 GPA
- Certified Payroll Professional (CPP) accredited and current

Figure 14.1: An example of the hybrid resume format.

Include Relevant Information About Your Background

Now that you've developed a keywords list, chosen a resume format, and decided on the top skills to emphasize, it's now time to begin plugging in pieces of your background. Review your three to five most important skills and ask yourself, "What experiences from my background and training provide evidence of my abilities in these areas?" Your examples may come from previous jobs, training classes you've taken, practice projects you've conducted on your own, or some other source. At this point, *all of your relevant experience counts.* Write a list of everything that comes to mind for each skill category, without judging whether or not it's a good piece of evidence.

Panic Point! You may be worrying that you don't have *any* evidence of your abilities in your new career area. This is a common and normal reaction, especially for Career Cowards. To overcome this panic, take a deep breath and say to yourself, "I may not be the most qualified person in this specialty (at least not *yet*), but I definitely have good things to offer. I will start small, listing tiny bits of my background, and build from there." Keep in mind that if you're truly panicking about what to include from your background, it can often be helpful to work with a professional skilled in writing career-change resumes. Their expertise can help you uncover pieces of your background that you never knew were relevant!

As a next step, decide which parts of your background you may want to include in your resume. Aim to choose three to five evidence statements for each of your three to five priority skill areas. Plug these sentences into your new resume to begin building the main portion of your new-you resume.

Focus on Functions Rather than Job Titles

For career-change resumes, it often makes sense to refer to your previous jobs in terms of their *function,* rather than their job titles. For instance, if your last two position titles were "Administrative Assistant," and you're aiming for a position as a meeting planner, consider highlighting a function or two from your previous job *rather* than a title. Check out the following "Before" and "After" examples.

Before:

- **Administrative Assistant,** ABC Company, 2005–Present

- **Administrative Assistant,** XYZ Corporation, 2003–2005

After:

- **Meeting Organization & Administration,** ABC Company, 2005–Present

- **Event Planning & Administration,** XYZ Corporation, 2003–2005

Referring to your *functions,* rather than your *job title,* allows you greater flexibility in presenting the new you into your new career.

Why It's Worth Doing

Hiring managers and decision makers are busy. When your resume finally lands in their hands, you'll have only a few seconds to catch their attention and convince them that they need to interview you. By taking the time now to create a customized, new-career resume, you greatly increase your chances of being taken seriously as a potential candidate in your new field—and moving forward toward making your career change a reality.

Career Champ Profile: Cindy

Cindy loved travel. Once her children were old enough for her to leave her part-time job working in the school district and return to work full time, Cindy wanted to become a part of the travel industry. Through her research, she discovered a career called Escape Planner, where specialists plan and organize trips for members of a travel club. Cindy loved the idea of becoming one herself and decided to build a resume highlighting her relevant background.

She began by researching keywords for similar jobs. It wasn't difficult; she input Escape Planner and Travel Specialist into www.monster.com and located several sample job descriptions, which she then compiled into a long list of keywords.

But then she started to panic. Did she truly have enough relevant experience to sell herself into an Escape Planner description? She pushed through her fear and made a list of parts of her background that would be relevant. She also changed her job titles to focus more on the functions she handled. When she put all of the pieces together, she felt much more confident about her ability to actually land a job in her dream career.

Figures 14.2 and 14.3 are examples of Cindy's "before" and "after" resumes.

Core Courage Concept

It's one thing to *say* you want to change careers, yet it's something very different to actually make it happen. Creating a resume that states in black and white what you have to offer in a new position is a brave step to take. What if you don't have enough evidence to make a good case for yourself? What if, even after you've done all this work, you still don't make progress toward your career-change goal?

While building a career-change resume is a scary step, you *can* do it. Take a deep breath and say to yourself, "I owe it to myself to keep plugging forward toward my dream. One step at a time is all it takes."

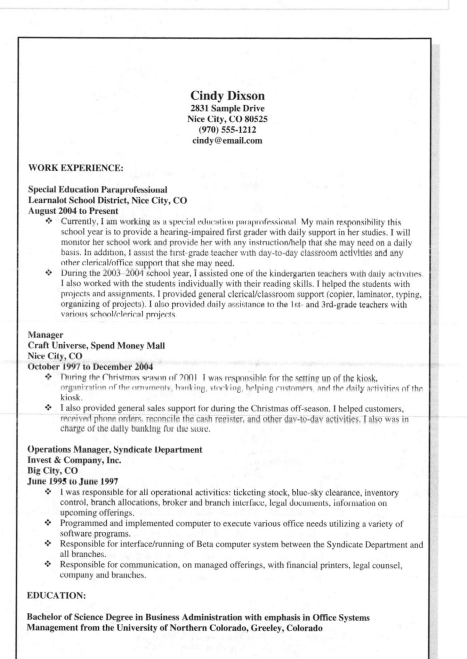

Cindy Dixson
2831 Sample Drive
Nice City, CO 80525
(970) 555-1212
cindy@email.com

WORK EXPERIENCE:

Special Education Paraprofessional
Learnalot School District, Nice City, CO
August 2004 to Present
- ❖ Currently, I am working as a special education paraprofessional. My main responsibility this school year is to provide a hearing-impaired first grader with daily support in her studies. I will monitor her school work and provide her with any instruction/help that she may need on a daily basis. In addition, I assist the first-grade teacher with day-to-day classroom activities and any other clerical/office support that she may need.
- ❖ During the 2003–2004 school year, I assisted one of the kindergarten teachers with daily activities. I also worked with the students individually with their reading skills. I helped the students with projects and assignments. I provided general clerical/classroom support (copier, laminator, typing, organizing of projects). I also provided daily assistance to the 1st- and 3rd-grade teachers with various school/clerical projects.

Manager
Craft Universe, Spend Money Mall
Nice City, CO
October 1997 to December 2004
- ❖ During the Christmas season of 2001 I was responsible for the setting up of the kiosk, organization of the ornaments, banking, stocking, helping customers, and the daily activities of the kiosk.
- ❖ I also provided general sales support for during the Christmas off-season. I helped customers, received phone orders, reconcile the cash register, and other day-to-day activities. I also was in charge of the daily banking for the store.

Operations Manager, Syndicate Department
Invest & Company, Inc.
Big City, CO
June 1995 to June 1997
- ❖ I was responsible for all operational activities: ticketing stock, blue-sky clearance, inventory control, branch allocations, broker and branch interface, legal documents, information on upcoming offerings.
- ❖ Programmed and implemented computer to execute various office needs utilizing a variety of software programs.
- ❖ Responsible for interface/running of Beta computer system between the Syndicate Department and all branches.
- ❖ Responsible for communication, on managed offerings, with financial printers, legal counsel, company and branches.

EDUCATION:

Bachelor of Science Degree in Business Administration with emphasis in Office Systems Management from the University of Northern Colorado, Greeley, Colorado

Figure 14.2: Cindy's "before" resume.

Cindy Dixson   *Escape Planner*
2831 Sample Drive
Nice City, CO 80525
(970) 555-1212, cindy@email.com

Effective Escape Planner with expertise arranging and coordinating travel and business
plans. Background in collecting detailed information, creating plans and reservations,
coordinating activities with service providers, working closely with clients, preparing reports and
e-mails, and confirming arrangements. Proven multitasker capable of effectively coordinating many
activities at once; level-headed performer able to resolve problems and find creative solutions for
last-minute challenges; excellent organizational and communication skills.

WORK EXPERIENCE

- **Client Support**   Learnalot School District   2004 to Present
- **Customer Service & Management**   Craft Universe   1997 to 2004
- **Customer Service & Administration**   Invest & Company, Inc.   1995 to 1997

Expertise in Member & Client Services

- Possess 5+ years experience in customer care roles, establishing effective working
  relationships, collecting and responding to critical information, and maintaining client data.
- Worked with high-end clientele in brokerage industry, managing and responding to thousands
  of client service details. Operated a highly organized and successful customer care operation
  and regularly received kudos for accuracy and professionalism.
- Expert in responding to and managing phone requests, orders, and reservations.
  Example: Kept a detailed database of contacts, deadlines, daily checklists, phone numbers,
  menu selections, hotel accommodations, and other detailed client information in order to
  respond to client needs in brokerage support position.
- Proven ability to effectively manage detailed expense and financial information, including
  preparing detailed summary reports.

Experience in Travel Planning, Organization & Attention to Detail

- Experienced in researching, planning, and creating computerized travel plans, made up of
  detailed day-by-day itineraries and "Wow!" experience options.
- Background in working effectively with local experts to discuss opportunities, make
  arrangements, and confirm reservations.
- Skilled in ensuring quality experiences by following up with service providers, resolving
  issues, and establishing systems and procedures to streamline future operations.
- Demonstrated ability to serve as back-up resource to respond to plan changes and emergency
  situations. Currently carry a cell phone to serve as backup resource when needed.

EDUCATION
Bachelor of Science Degree in Business Administration with emphasis in
Office Systems Management from the University of Northern Colorado, Greeley, Colorado

Figure 14.3: Cindy's "after" resume.

Confidence Checklist

☐ Build a strong foundation with a list of keywords.

☐ Pick the best resume format for your needs.

☐ Include relevant information about your background.

☐ Focus on functions rather than job titles.

Chapter 15

Land Your First New-Career Position

Finally, you're ready to officially step into your new specialty. All the hard work you've done to define, research, choose, and prepare for your new career is about to pay off. The following powerful job search strategies (achievable for even Career Cowards!) will help you land your first great new-career position.

Risk It or Run From It?

- **Risk Rating:** Mid-to-high risk range. (Putting yourself in front of possible employers can feel a bit scary.)

- **Payoff Potential:** Fantastic! Here's where you have the power to make your career-change dreams a reality.

- **Time to Complete:** Typically, job search takes about one month for every $10,000 in income you hope to earn, so you do the calculation.

- **Bailout Strategy:** Well, you can hope that a job will come knocking on your door, but you may be waiting a long, long time for that to happen. A better plan would be to implement some of the activities described in this chapter that feel doable to you.

(continued)

(continued)

> • **The "20 Percent Extra" Edge:** Most job searchers (about 90 percent, in fact) will wait for a position to be advertised, and then apply. Executing the activities recommended in this chapter will open up many more exciting job possibilities for you—and you won't have to wait for an ad.
>
> • **"Go For It!" Bonus Activity:** Throw a new-career launch party and invite many of your supporters. Post your resume, target list, and notepaper around the room, and ask attendees to jot notes about ideas and resources they have to help you land your first new-career position.

How to Find Your First New-Career Position

There are endless exciting opportunities available in the world of work—many of them within the new-career field you're targeting. The following effective job search activities will help you find the right one for you.

Define Your Target Employers

You're ready to land your first position in your new career. A first step toward finding great opportunities is to ask yourself, "Who would be likely to hire me for this kind of work?" Answer this question, and your job search will be off to a great start. Knowing which organizations are most likely to hire people in your specialty will help you be much more efficient and successful with your search activities.

Make use of these resources to identify your list of potential employers:

- **The phone book Yellow Pages section:** Look up the names of companies listed in the industry categories that pertain to your work.

- **Business directories and databases:** Head to your local library (or access the resources online) and check out any directories or databases that pertain to your industry or career focus areas. Ask the reference librarian for help if you're not sure where to look.

- **Membership lists:** Remember those professional associations you checked into when you were finding specialists for informational interviews? Those same groups often publish a list of members and the companies where they work. These lists are excellent target-employer resources.

A few things to keep in mind as you develop your list of possible hiring companies:

- Make sure you consider small organizations as well as larger ones. Many job searchers naturally think about bigger employers as potential places to work, yet most of us (75 percent, in fact!) are employed at companies with fewer than 25 employees. So as you consider potential employers, be sure to include smaller businesses as well.

- Aim to create a list of 20 to 50 potential employers. That may sound like a lot, but it's better to have several possible employers to target than to start with a very small list. If you're having trouble coming up with enough companies, look at industries that are related to the kind of work you want to do. An interior designer, for instance, could work for design firms as well as construction companies, furniture stores, flooring businesses, and so on.

Once you've developed your initial list, begin to create a research file on these organizations. Aim to learn what they do, who's in charge, and how to contact them. The Internet, directories, and local publications can help you locate information about each potential employer.

Plan an Effective Job Search Strategy

Typically, Career Cowards aren't effective job searchers. They, along with 9 out of 10 other job searchers, usually wait for a job to be advertised before taking any action. Putting yourself out there more directly can seem too scary, right?

Yet consider this: Most jobs (almost 70 percent!) *never get advertised.* That means that 90 percent of job searchers go after only 30 percent of the jobs. In fact, it's not unusual for 200 or 300 applicants to apply to a single opening. Talk about setting yourself up for some stiff competition!

Even though it may feel a little scary, consider using more effective job search activities to greatly increase your chances for finding a great new-career position. The following job search avenues were reported in "Getting a Job," by Mark S. Granovetter, a Harvard University researcher, to be the most effective (and I've also seen this data to be true through my own 15 years of career counseling experiences):

- **Apply directly to employers, even if no opening is posted.** Referred to as "direct application," one third of jobs are found through this method. Direct application involves sending a resume and cover letter to a hiring manager or stopping by to drop off a resume.

- **Network to uncover opportunities.** An additional one third of job openings get filled through the "who you know" system. Even though networking seems scary—especially to Career Cowards—there are easy, less risky activities you can use. It's the tried-and-proven "who you know is more important than what you know" approach.

- **Respond to job ads.** Although the final one third of positions are filled through this activity, keep in mind that 90 percent of job hunters rely on this avenue as their only job search activity. This makes for huge competition and fewer overall results for you.

As you develop your new-career job search plan, aim to include activities from direct application, networking, *and* responding to ads, to create a balanced, effective job search strategy.

Apply Directly to Potential Employers

You know that target list you just finished developing? A simple and *very* effective job search activity is to send your resume and a cover letter to a contact at all the companies on your list. What should your letter say? Figure 15.1 is an example of a direct-application cover letter.

Elle du West   **Business Services Coordinator**

412 Sample Street
Great City, CO 80555
(970) 555-1212
elleduwest@email.com

Organized, Effective, Personable

DATE

NAME AND
ADDRESS OF
POTENTIAL
EMPLOYER

Dear Decision Maker,

    I am writing to express interest in any current or future **Business Services Support** opportunities available within your organization. Following are highlights of my background as they may pertain to your needs:

Proven Ability to Manage Projects Effectively

• There have been many instances in my career where I have planned and executed detailed projects, such as process improvement projects, large scale events, etc.
• In all cases, the results have been excellent: Projects were completed on time, to established specifications, with better-than-expected results.
• Additionally, I have been able to create productive long-term relationships with suppliers and customers, leading to win-win outcomes for everyone involved.

Customer Service & Teamwork Expertise

• My background includes advanced training in cultivating positive relationships. These skills support my successful interactions with coworkers and customers.
• I possess the ability to remain calm and think logically in stressful situations. This strength has allowed me to effectively resolve problems and achieve goals.

    Your organization is of interest to me, and I would welcome the opportunity to talk with you further about your needs and my background. In the next few days, I will follow up with you to confirm receipt of these materials, and to determine a logical next step.

    Thank you in advance for your consideration of my qualifications and interest.

Sincerely,

Elle du West

Figure 15.1: A direct-application cover letter.

The letter you develop should contain the following pieces of essential information:

- **Your contact information:** Name, address, e-mail, phone.

- **Your new career target:** This can simply be the job title for the career you're pursuing.

- **A few highlights about your background as it pertains to your new career:** Feel free to repeat a few sentences from the information you included in your resume. Repeating it twice helps the employer notice it more!

- **What you want to have happen next:** Either say that you'll contact them, as Elle did in this example, or include a line such as, "Please contact me to arrange a time for us to talk." (Note: You contacting them is *much* more effective than waiting for them to contact you!)

That's it! Once you've written your direct-application cover letter, mail it along with your new-career resume to contacts on your target list. Not sure who to send it to? If you can, it's best to include a person's name. Often you can find this information online or in directories. If you're not able to locate a specific name, "Director of FUNCTION" (filling in the appropriate role, such as "Sales" or "Client Services") is a reasonable substitute.

Panic Point! Is your cowardice at its peak right now, thinking about sending your resume to potential employers? You're not alone. Direct application strikes fear in even the bravest of job searchers because you're putting yourself out there for the world to accept or reject. It's scary! Yet consider this: One third of all jobs come from direct application, *yet only about 10 percent of job searchers ever even try it.* Your odds of success are really pretty high! To help yourself overcome your direct-application fears, ask yourself, "What's the worst that could happen?" Your letter may wind up in the trash.

> Could you live with that? Then think about the best that could happen...the chance to land a great job in your new career field. Is it worth the risk? You decide!

If sending out lots of direct-application letters scares you, start small. Mail three letters a week over a few months. And refer to some of the techniques described in chapters 8 and 9 to help you with following up on your letters and getting unstuck.

After you've mailed them, if you do decide to follow up, use a script such as this:

> "Mr. Employer, my name is [YOUR NAME]. I'm following up on a letter and resume I sent a few days ago. I'd like a chance to come in to introduce myself. Would you have time either Thursday or Friday afternoon to meet with me for 15 minutes or so?"

Be aware: Most hiring managers will respond to your request with, "But we're not hiring right now." Don't let this answer derail you. Be prepared to reply with a response like this:

> "That's fine. I'd still like to meet you anyway. Things may change in the future and it would be good for us to know each other. Could we schedule a brief meeting?"

Let Other People Help You

You may not realize it, but over the last few months you've most likely developed a group of supporters who can help you land your first position in your new career. Remember the specialists you interviewed about their work? The professional association members you contacted for ideas? The instructors who helped you train for your new career? And you probably also know a number of other people who may be able to provide assistance.

Each of the individuals in your network has the potential to help you achieve your next career-change goal. How should you make the best use of your network? Begin by making a list of everyone you know, professionally and personally.

Panic Point! Embarrassed to let your friends, family, colleagues, and acquaintances know that you're job searching? That's a common Career Coward concern. But relax. For now, you just need to put their name on a list. Later, you can decide whether you want to contact them.

If you do decide to make use of networking in your job search (and tap into another 30 percent of the available job opportunities), send some of your contacts your new-career resume along with a short, handwritten note like this:

Dear [CONTACT NAME],

I'm job searching, and I've enclosed a resume for you to review. Would you be willing to brainstorm some next steps with me? I'll contact you in the next few days to see if we can set up a time to talk. Thank you for your consideration of my request.

Sincerely,

[YOUR NAME]

Or, if you don't want to meet (because it seems too scary), your note could say this:

Dear [CONTACT NAME],

I'm job searching, and I've enclosed a resume for you to review. Would you please keep me in mind if you hear of any opportunities related to my career goals? Thank you in advance for any support you can offer.

Sincerely,

[YOUR NAME]

If you do end up meeting with some of your contacts, be sure to show them your target list of potential employers and ask them for ideas on next steps, but avoid asking the, "Do you know of any job for me?" question. It's too direct!

Why It's Worth Doing

Most job searchers don't know how to job search effectively, and find themselves in the trap of waiting for and responding to highly competitive posted job ads. Yet you now know better ways to locate exciting new-career opportunities. You can choose to stay in the job-ad rut, or you can significantly improve your chances for finding and landing a great new career position simply by taking advantage of direct application and networking activities. If those job search activities seem scary, look beyond the step of *finding* a great new-career position and picture yourself enjoying and succeeding in your new career. Is it worth it to take some risks to get there? You decide.

Career Champ Profile: Elle

Elle was taking steps to shift from her work as a substance-abuse counselor into a career as a concierge—a specialist who would coordinate a variety of personal and business services for clients. Elle had researched the concierge field and determined that it was a good fit for her. She'd then created a new-career resume, prepared for job interviews, and was now about to send her resume to potential employers. But the idea of direct application *terrified* her!

For three weeks in a row, she told me that she was going to send out a few direct-application mailings. And for three weeks in a row, she didn't do it. "I know I should, but I'm just so scared," she confessed. "I'm afraid they're going to laugh at me and throw my resume in the trash." "They might," I agreed. "Could you live with that?" Elle thought for a few seconds. "You know, I could live with that. I'm so excited about getting started in this new line of work that I'm willing to take the risk of being laughed at and rejected."

Deciding to take a small risk, Elle mailed two direct-application packages to potential employers the next day. I phoned her a few days later to check in: "In your cover letter, did you say that you'd follow up?" I asked. "Yes…" she replied hesitantly, "so now I need to call them, don't I?" We both laughed, remembering how difficult it had been for Elle to make phone calls requesting informational interviews. "But I'll do what I did before," she said, already seeming more upbeat. "I can send an e-mail first, and the next day I can call after hours to leave a voice mail. And I'll use a script; that really helped me last time. I can do it!" she said, with excitement in her voice.

The next morning when I checked my voice mail, there was a message from Elle. "You won't believe this," she began. "A few hours after I talked to you I got a call from the owner of one of the concierge companies where I'd sent my direct-application materials. He said he wanted to meet me—that they might need to hire someone new in the next month or so. I have an interview with him tomorrow. I'm really nervous, but I'm super-excited, too!"

In the end, Elle had three interviews with the concierge company and was offered a job. Her new career had begun!

Core Courage Concept

You can wait (and wait, and *wait*) for an exciting new-career opportunity to land in your lap. But it may take a long, long time—if it ever happens at all. Yet consider all of the brave steps you've accomplished so far: defining and researching a new career field, choosing one and getting trained, and developing a resume that presents the new you. Even though it can seem *very* scary to put yourself out there, you *can* do it—to keep moving forward toward making your career-change goals come true.

Confidence Checklist

☐ Define your target employers.

☐ Plan an effective job search strategy.

☐ Apply directly to potential employers.

☐ Let other people help you.

Chapter 16

Present the New You Effectively in Job Interviews

Soon you'll have the chance to talk with potential employers about what you have to offer in your new career. And you'll want to be prepared. The steps outlined in this chapter will help you feel ready to effectively promote yourself into your new specialty (and if you're looking for even more great ideas, check out my first book, *The Career Coward's Guide to Interviewing*).

Risk It or Run From It?

- **Risk Rating:** No real risk in the preparation. Just brainstorming and practicing with yourself.

- **Payoff Potential:** Very high. The work you do here can help open doors to your career future.

- **Time to Complete:** About the time it would take you to get through a good movie.

- **Bailout Strategy:** You can try and "wing it" in an interview, and sell yourself on your charm alone. If you're good at that, it might work. Otherwise, a little interview preparation probably wouldn't hurt.

(continued)

(continued)

> - **The "20 Percent Extra" Edge:** You're convinced that you can succeed in your chosen career. Learning how to effectively present evidence of your skills and background to a potential employer will speed up the time it takes for you to land your first job in your new career.
>
> - **"Go For It!" Bonus Activity:** Go through a few videotaped mock interviews. Your local job service center may offer this service, or ask a supporter to help you practice.

How to Convince an Employer (and Yourself) That You've Got What It Takes

You're moving closer and closer to making your career change a reality. Move a step closer to your goals by making sure that you present yourself effectively in your interviews. The following steps will show you how.

Master a Few Great Stories to Tell

Imagine walking into an interview feeling confident because you know that in your pocket, you have concrete evidence of what you have to offer to an employer. Develop that confidence-building pocketful of proof with the following activities:

- **Brainstorm several examples of your background as it relates to your new work.** You may have already completed this step when you gathered examples for your career-change resume. Look over your lists of key skills and examples you developed in chapter 14 for ideas.

- **Develop your examples into stories you can share in an interview.** The What, How, and Proof format offers an easy-to-remember, effective way to promote yourself: *What* was the challenge or opportunity you were facing, *How* did you respond to it, and what *Proof* do you have that you succeeded? Here's an example a candidate might share if he was working toward landing a job in nonprofit fund-raising:

- *What:* A local elementary school needed to raise $10,000 to buy some new computer equipment for the media center. I was put in charge of handling that fund-raising project.

- *How:* I began by researching several possible fund-raising activities and talked with other schools that had used them. Ultimately, I decided on a combination of two activities: silent-auction parties held in each classroom, and corporate donation requests made to local businesses. I developed and implemented detailed plans for these activities and coordinated the efforts of 40 volunteers over a period of three months.

- *Proof:* Overall, the fund-raising effort was a huge success. We raised $4,000 through the classroom silent auctions, and $7,000 from corporate donations, so we were able to exceed our goal!

Panic Point! Worried that your stories won't be interesting or important enough to make a good impression? Keep in mind that even though your story may seem insignificant to you, it will provide the employer with some concrete evidence of your abilities. He or she isn't looking for *tons* of evidence—just enough to feel confident in taking a risk on you. So don't discount your examples too quickly. They're valuable!

Aim to come up with at least five stories that emphasize your ability to succeed in your new career. Remember, you can pull examples from practice projects, volunteer work, classes you've taken, or experiences in your former positions. It all counts! Once you've identified these stories, practice them out loud several times. The practice will improve your presentation skills while greatly increasing your confidence.

Create a Comforting "Security Blanket" Portfolio

In addition to the concrete-evidence examples you just developed, consider creating a portfolio of your new-career expertise. Your portfolio can take many forms: a slim binder of pictures and documents, a Web page with images and descriptions, or a briefcase of show-and-tell items. Choose the format that works best for you and fill it with 5 to 10 items (no more than that, or the interviewer may lose interest) relevant to your new career. These might include

- Letters of appreciation from happy customers

- Pictures or samples of your work

- A certificate of training

- Samples of literature or documents

- Performance reviews

- Anything else you can think of that will help you prove your case

During the interview, be on the lookout for opportunities to share an item in your portfolio. Often, *showing* an example has a much greater impact than simply *telling* someone about it. Plus, knowing that you have that concrete evidence at your side is almost as good as having a security blanket!

Keep Your Focus on Your Future Career

There you sit, excited (and a little nervous) to be interviewing for a position in your new career field. You're dying to tell the hiring manager about the process you went through to choose this specialty—to help her see how truly excited you are to be changing careers. But before you launch into sharing this exciting adventure, consider this: The hiring manager's top priority is to choose someone capable of doing the job. By telling your career-change story in detail—about how you used to do one kind of work, and now you want to be involved in this new work—you may instead weaken the decision maker's belief in your abilities. You don't want the employer thinking, "Hmmm…this guy seems to be too much of a newbie…."

It's probably wiser to share the detailed account of your career-change adventure with friends, but not with a potential employer. With the hiring manager, you'll instead want to emphasize the experience and skills you offer relevant to the position. If you catch yourself about to say something like, "Well, because this is a brand-new career for me, I haven't had much experience in that yet," shift your response to something like, "I have experience in that area. Let me give you an example…."

Why It's Worth Doing

Does getting ready for an interview seem like a tedious waste of time to you? Won't your enthusiasm and charm be enough to sell you into the job? Or maybe you're feeling nervous that an employer will see right through your lack of experience: Do you truly have enough to offer?

Whichever side of the fence you're on, going through the steps of preparing some examples and creating a portfolio of relevant items gives you a solid foundation for presenting yourself effectively in interviews. A few hours invested in preparation now can significantly speed up the time it takes to land an exciting new-career position.

Career Champ Profile: Lyndall

Lyndall sat across from Sue at the coffee shop. Sue was looking for an assistant for her home-care-services business. Lyndall had chosen home care coordinator as her new career path after interviewing four other specialists, job shadowing one of them, and conducting her own practice project helping her friend find home care services for her friend's mother. Lyndall had also taken a one-day course in home care coordination to help her get prepared for her new career.

"Have you ever worked as a home care coordinator before?" Sue asked her. Lyndall had dreaded this question, afraid that Sue would think of her as an imposter. She was about to say, "No, I never have worked as a home care coordinator before," but then caught herself and responded with this answer: "Yes, in fact, I've brought a letter from a client for whom I coordinated home-care services for her mother," Lyndall replied, opening a slim portfolio containing the letter. "This was an interesting project," Lyndall began. She then told Sue about her client (she didn't describe her as her "friend") and the home-care needs of her mother. "I located and organized several great resources, using the information and techniques I learned in a Home Care Coordination course I took recently," Lyndall continued, flipping to another page in her portfolio showing her course certificate.

Sue looked impressed. "Lyndall, would you be able to come by my office next Tuesday at noon? I'll order in some lunch and we can talk about a next step for working together."

Core Courage Concept

You need to convince an employer that you've got what it takes to succeed in your new line of work...*and*, even more importantly, you need to convince yourself! Going through the steps of developing and practicing examples, and creating a portfolio of concrete evidence, allows you to build your confidence step by step. Then, when the interview begins, you'll be ready!

Confidence Checklist

☐ Master a few great stories to tell.

☐ Create a comforting "security blanket" portfolio.

☐ Keep your focus on your future career.

Chapter 17

Succeed and Progress in Your New Career

Y ou're in! Your life in your new career has begun. Now you have the power to steer the course of your new career in increasingly satisfying directions using the achievement and advancement techniques described in this chapter.

Risk It or Run From It?

- **Risk Rating:** Pretty high. Now that you're working in your new-career field, your performance and actions will impact your successes or failures.

- **Payoff Potential:** Considerable. Handle this first new-career job effectively and you can advance further, faster, into the work you love to do.

- **Time to Complete:** Weeks, months, years…career progress is an ongoing project. Yet the journey—especially within a field that you love—can be awesome.

- **Bailout Strategy:** You can let your new career "just happen," with no real plan. Most people manage their careers that way, and it works okay for some of them. Yet most people without a career plan end up feeling aimless and

---

(continued)

(continued)

> frustrated after a while. It would probably be worth it to at least scope out a career-development strategy and then later decide whether you want to implement it.
>
> - **The "20 Percent Extra" Edge:** The "man with the plan" is almost always in a better position than the one without. Knowing how you want to progress in your career allows you to better identify and take advantage of opportunities.
>
> - **"Go For It!" Bonus Activity:** Read biographies of successful people to gain ideas and insight for how you can achieve extraordinary career results.

How to Succeed and Progress in Your New Career

You probably feel a little shaky now, getting started in your new specialty. Yet in your heart you know that once you master this position, your passion and interests will drive you to attain positions of even greater responsibility and challenge. Learn how to succeed through the new-job jitters, while keeping your eyes on opportunities for the future.

Allow Yourself to Experience New-Job Jitters and Frustration

I'll never forget my first day as a career counselor: There I sat at my big desk wearing the "right" clothes (a proper navy suit, white blouse, and uncomfortable pumps), my pen in hand ready to take notes, staring across the desk at my first client, an angry 40-something gentleman who had been laid off from his job as a manufacturing manager—and he was itching to land his next one. "What am I *doing*?" I remember thinking to myself. "I don't have a clue how to help this guy. Any second now he's going to see what an imposter I am and demand that I be fired."

Then the words of one of my career-counseling instructors popped into my head: "You only need to be a little bit ahead of where your client is in his or her process. You don't need to know everything. If you're not sure about the answer to something, simply say, 'I'd like to research that and get back to you with more information.'" Her words saved me from having a total nervous breakdown in front of that client, and somehow I made it through that first session.

Although it wasn't smooth sailing from then on, I did become much more comfortable in my new role after the first three weeks. Experts say 21 days is about how long it takes to settle into a new routine or habit. Within that time I found out where the restroom was located, how to request office supplies, and what would happen if I didn't have the answer to a client's request (I did just what my instructor suggested: Told my clients I'd find out and then get back to them — and it worked out okay).

But there were also plenty of panic moments during that time — instances when I'd say to myself, "Oh no! I think I made the wrong career choice!" But I'd take a deep breath and then tell myself, "Be patient. I need time to settle in. If I decide down the line that this isn't right for me, I'll adjust my plan."

It's very likely that at the start of your first new-career position, you'll go through many moments of panic, too. Reassure yourself that it's normal to feel confused and scared for a while as you begin a new experience.

Panic Point! What if you start your new position and then discover that it's the wrong fit for you? As with any new job, you may get the feeling early on that something is off base. Rather than run away in panic, spend some time diagnosing the problem. Are you overwhelmed because you don't yet know how to do the work? Or frustrated because your assignments seem too simple for you? Both of these problems will most likely resolve themselves over time, as you gain mastery or get promoted into work that's a better fit for your experience.

(continued)

(continued)

> If, however, you determine that your employer is impossible to work for (there are plenty of dysfunctional workplaces out there!), it's probably best to cut your losses and begin looking for work with a different employer.

Develop a Career-Progress Plan

As you settle into your first new-career position, chances are you'll begin to wonder, "Where will I take my career from here?" Your first new-career opportunity will allow you to build some experience and confidence, and then you'll probably want to move on to another opportunity after a period of time. So where will you want to take your career from here?

You may already have a good idea of your future career plans. As you conducted your career research, it's likely that you learned about specialties and positions that fit your long-term career objectives. If not, consider conducting more informational interviews and career experiments to identify future career aims that will be inspiring for you. Having a picture of where you want to take your career will help you determine which steps to take to get there.

For example, after I'd worked for a year with a national career-management company, I began to think about having my own career-counseling practice. I wanted more freedom to create and deliver services helpful to my clients—independence I didn't have working for someone else. Once I'd decided to pursue the goal of having my own practice, I realized that I'd need to learn how to run a business, as well as how to become an outstanding career counselor, so that my reputation would attract clients. Those objectives gave me a focus for my learning over the next two years, and then I opened my own business.

Where do you want to take your career from here? And what will you need to learn and accomplish to get there? Your answers to these two questions can serve as the foundation for your new-career-development plan. Build in specifics such as training and experiences you'll need to obtain, and people and organizations that can help accomplish those goals. Write out the steps you've identified, realizing that you can modify this plan as your interests develop and opportunities evolve.

Take Small Risks That Lead to Big Career Results

Now that you have a basic career-development plan, wish you could fast-forward through the steps? Although a career-development time machine hasn't yet been developed, you do have the power to speed up your career progress by taking small (yet high-payoff) risks. The following activities can help increase the pace of your progress:

- **Share your career-development plan with your boss, mentors, and other supporters in your life.** Once others know what you're aiming to accomplish, they can be on the lookout for possibilities and ways to help.

- **Review your career-development plan at least once each month.** Look at the steps and ask yourself, "What can I be doing right now that will help me move forward?" Oftentimes, there are opportunities ripe for the picking if you keep your focus on your goals.

- **Be creative and flexible.** Need to learn a certain skill to be qualified for the next step along your career path? Consider seeking out extra assignments—even if you may not be paid for them—in order to master a new technique and gain valuable experience.

- **Take reasonable risks.** Even though it may make your heart pound, contact influential people in your career field and request networking meetings. Learn about their career histories and ask for their ideas to help you accomplish your own goals. And whenever possible (even if it costs money to participate), attend association meetings and conferences. Establish yourself as a leader in your field by volunteering for community and professional activities.

Even though you may still feel insecure, taking small steps to grow outside of your comfort zone will go a long way toward expanding your opportunities and accelerating your results.

Maintain Long-Term Career Health

We all have a tendency to "settle into" a career situation (like a comfy easy chair), especially if it's a job that we like. Yet you know as well as I do that jobs don't last forever. Markets shift, companies change, and new leadership takes over. For these reasons, it's essential to stay active in maintaining your career health, especially if you're looking forward to a long, happy life in your new specialty. These simple steps will help you keep your new career in tip-top shape:

- **Build and grow a strong professional network.** Keep in touch with the contacts you've made through your field research, during job search networking, and in your new position. Take an interest in their careers and lives, and connect with them once or twice each year. As your careers evolve, you can be important supporters for one another.

- **Maintain current career skills.** An up-to-date skill set will position you as someone dedicated to excellence in your work. State-of-the-art skills will also help you move more easily from one great job opportunity to the next.

- **Regularly reevaluate your career satisfaction.** You've worked hard to get to this point: You researched, chose, and moved into a career field that's more satisfying for you. Yet as you continue to grow and develop, your interests and needs will change. Make use of the career strategies you've mastered in this book—regularly reevaluating your values, interests, skills, and talents—to implement career changes that keep you on course for a lifetime of outstanding career results.

Why It's Worth Doing

Sure, you can skate along without a career-development plan; most people do! Yet since you've already done so much work to arrive at a better place in your career, why not keep the momentum going? Without conscious attention to taking your career in an increasingly successful direction, you stand the chance of falling into a rut—and ending up dissatisfied and unhappy once again. A bit of planning and investing in yourself along the way will help you create a lifetime of career happiness and success.

Career Champ Profile: Len

Len successfully switched careers from managing an auto-parts store to recruiting new employees for high-tech companies. He began his new career as a junior recruiter with an employment agency, but determined pretty quickly that he'd like to move up. His longer-term career goal was to land a position as an on-staff recruiter with one of the large technology companies in his area, knowing that the pay, benefits, and career opportunities would be better.

Motivated to make his career goal a reality, Len joined and became an active participant in three professional organizations: a human resources society, a technical recruiters group, and a chamber association. Although he was still mastering the recruiting specialty, he took small risks and volunteered for committees and projects that allowed him to learn new skills and connect with others in his profession.

Eighteen months later, Len heard about an on-staff recruiting opening at one of his target technology companies. It turned out that he was already acquainted with the hiring manager because they'd worked together on a human resources society event. Len successfully landed that job.

For the next year, Len continued to actively participate in his professional organization activities, while also working toward a Professional in Human Resources certification. Right after completing it, he received a call from a colleague tipping him off to a recruiting manager opening at another of Len's target companies. Len interviewed for and landed that position.

Within three years of beginning his new career, Len had quadrupled his earnings from his first new-career position, and was living the career life he'd envisioned years ago—challenged, and happier than he'd ever been before!

Core Courage Concept

Wow...if you haven't yet recognized the courage you've demonstrated so far, let me do it for you: Congratulations! Now that you're involved in a career you love, you'll want to keep progressing. *Go for it*. And when you hit a panic point in your new career, remember all that you've accomplished already. You have the talent and motivation to succeed again and again and again. Here's wishing you a lifetime of career success and happiness—you're making it a reality one courageous step after another!

Confidence Checklist

☐ Allow yourself to experience new-job jitters and frustration.

☐ Develop a career progress plan.

☐ Take small risks that lead to big career results.

☐ Maintain long-term career health.

Index